NICHING UP

THE NARROWER
THE MARKET,
THE BIGGER THE PRIZE

NICHING UP

CHRIS DREYER

LIONCREST
PUBLISHING

NICHING UP

The Narrower the Market, the Bigger the Prize

FIRST EDITION

ISBN   978-1-5445-3243-1 *Hardcover*

       978-1-5445-3242-4 *Paperback*

       978-1-5445-3244-8 *Ebook*

       978-1-5445-3245-5 *Audiobook*

FOR GREY,

I LOVE YOU, SON.

CONTENTS

INTRODUCTION

Anything I've been successful at can be attributed, in some way, to niching.

In 2006, I started doing affiliate marketing as a side hustle from my full-time job as a basketball coach and detention supervisor. The very first website I made was loseadoublechin.com. It started out as sort of a joke, but the reality behind it is that I was overwhelmed by the thought of tackling the diet and weight loss industry. I didn't feel secure in my knowledge, not being a physician or having a medical background, or about learning such a broad and complicated topic. On the other hand, chins are just a small part of the body, and I thought I could learn enough about this one area by reading as much information as possible.

So I created this site and I soon ranked number one for "double chin" on Google. It was a terrible site, but it ranked number one for several years. It was quite successful, and it made a lot of money.

Then I started thinking, "This one site did so well and it's not even my best work. I bet I can do this again!"

I ended up making eighty other websites. I earned a hundred dollars here, two hundred bucks there, but nothing like the success of the double chin site. My first mistake—reflecting on this many years in the future—was that I didn't appreciate what I had done right. I had niched!

I should have realized what worked and run with it.

When I decided to start my digital marketing agency, I initially launched attorneyrankings.org (though we are now rankings. io). I knew I wanted to work in the legal industry, but I was scared that every time I gave up a service, it would hurt my revenue or my positioning. In actuality, every time I chose to not do one thing, other doors opened. I discovered a propensity for search engine optimization (SEO), and I started to find more success.

When I went to Vistage (which is a peer advisory group for CEOs) and had my first business review, I was told, "You need to offer your services to physicians, home services, and these other niches, because you're doing so well with legal."

I didn't take my own advice or learn from my previous experience with all those affiliate sites. Instead I listened to my peers (who, in retrospect, were in industries that were completely different from mine) and went after a larger cap.

I signed a dental practice and a few other clients in other niches—and my momentum slowed. I had more people to sell to, but I was growing at a slower pace. If you've seen those stock market charts with the zig-zag arrow showing ups and downs, this was a big red arrow pointing downward. I kept asking myself, "What's going on?"

As you've probably guessed, I had severely discounted my positioning as an expert when I was only specializing in legal.

Thankfully I didn't stay on this path too long. We fixed our positioning, and the arrow started pointing upward again.

This time I learned—so well, in fact, that niching as a provider of SEO specifically to personal injury attorneys has contributed to our company being an Inc 5000 recipient for the past five years in a row.

I also learned that anything I've ever been successful at is because I've been obsessively focused. I won fourth place in a 14,000-player poker tournament because I focused on nothing else for a whole month and reviewed 40,000 hands of poker during that time. I was a top-rated collectible card player because there were many clans to play, but I learned the ins and outs of just a few. In sports, I was successful because I focused on basketball, went to summer basketball camp, and put all my hours and attention into training for just basketball. That focus led to me becoming captain of our conference and being offered scholarships to play college basketball.

I'll tell these stories in more detail later, but for now suffice it to say that I owe my success to *niching up*.

DOESN'T NICHING MEAN SAYING NO?

Every time I've considered niching up, it feels like stepping off a cliff. It's scary at first—*what if I don't know what I'm doing? What if I fail?* But every time I've taken that step, it ends up being a really positive decision.

Why? Because niching up means moving forward from a place of abundance and growth.

The first thing many people think of when they hear niching is scarcity; they think of having fewer opportunities, of less ability to monetize or grow their business, of *taking something away.* Many individuals' biggest fear with niching is that by saying yes to one area, they're saying no to many others. It's true: niching does mean saying no to business and shrinking your market. For example, for me to become a standout basketball player, I had to focus on that one sport—which meant I had to quit practicing baseball as much.

But in reality, niching provides opportunities and gives you *optionality.* Even after you choose a niche, if you get a lead that's not where your deep expertise lies, you don't have to say no. In many cases you will, because it's not your main focus, but you always have the option of saying yes if it's an opportunity you particularly want to explore. In some cases, you can genuinely help with something that's not specific to your niche, so you don't have to look at it only as black or white, yes or no.

By saying no to some things, niching opens the door to many things—including more or better possibilities.

And that knowledge—that you don't have to slam the door shut on other business opportunities just because you choose to niche up—takes away some of that fear. I find it reassuring to know that just because I choose to focus on helping personal injury attorneys with SEO, that doesn't mean no other opportunities can ever come through my door. In reality, I do mostly personal injury (PI) but I have the option of saying yes to something else if it makes sense for me.

In fact, of my forty-five current clients, I have three that are not personal injury attorneys. Three may not be a lot, but that's three times I said yes outside my niche.

Most recently, I had a divorce attorney come to me and say, "Let's rock and roll!"

I knew I could serve and help them—their keywords and SEO strategy are similar, and they had the right attitude—so I said yes. But that doesn't mean that I'm going to now market myself for both PI *and* divorce law SEO.

Far from narrowing your options, niching up opens a world of possibility to say yes to the people who are right for you and your business—the ones you are best suited to help.

RICHES ARE IN THE NICHES

Telling stories has always been my go-to method for teaching.

I've spun tales for high schoolers about how an underdog hoops upstart was able to join the first string through good choices and hard work. I've doled out yarns to website visitors about extreme double-chin reduction achieved through clean eating and exercise regimes. And, through the stories in this book, I hope I am able to help you learn from my journey with niching—both from my mistakes and what I got right.

Along the way, I'll help you to see your own existing business, or the business you dream of founding, through the niching lens. You'll understand the many benefits niching can offer, and how it can be easily applied to any business vertical. You'll learn how to figure out if niching is right for you simply by determining who it is that you are able to serve best and most efficiently. Finally, I'll show you that you don't need to undertake a ton of research or spend money to do any of it. You already collect all of the data that you'll need.

When you choose a specialization, your focus and attention make all the difference. Niching allows you to stand out, to be in a blue ocean instead of a red one. And when you niche up, you obtain significant advantages.

That doesn't mean that there are no downsides, just that everything you gain through niching outweighs those disadvantages. In fact, we'll address the potential cons of niching in Chapter 1, and the rest of the chapters will show you all the benefits of niching up—things like:

- having greater *awareness* of the opportunities open to you, so you can choose where to say yes or no;
- gaining *expertise* through hours of practice, which sets you apart in your field;
- being able to charge *premium prices* because people feel you've invested more time in becoming an expert and therefore they're willing to pay more for it;

- more easily *converting* prospects to clients because you better understand your niche audience;
- having better *relationships* with those in your industry, which leads to more goodwill;
- getting—and giving—more *referrals*, which means helping more people;
- and becoming more *efficient* as you develop repeatable processes designed to help you and your clients.

Let me be clear that niching is not for everyone and this book is not my attempt to convince you that every business ought to serve a niche audience. If you're a business owner who is happy with your margins and the manner in which you're competing, perhaps you'll read this book and still decide to stick with what's working. I've seen niching make a positive difference for entrepreneurs who sell everything from Facebook ads to baskets of fries, but I'm not arrogant enough to believe that I know what's best for every business. I'm just sharing my experience with niching, how it's benefited me, and how I think it may be able to benefit you, too.

This book is also not a step-by-step guide to finding your specific niche. Every niching decision is unique, so while I can absolutely give you a primer on the facts and figures you should pull together in order to figure it out, I can't make the determination for you. By the time you're finished reading you'll be armed with all you need to reach your own conclusions.

I'm excited to invite you along on my journey, and I can't wait for you to understand why I believe so deeply that, for most businesses, the niches hold your riches.

CHAPTER 1

↓

ATTACK OF THE CONS

The first time I watched *Star Wars: Episode II - Attack of the Clones*, I immediately noticed something different about one of the lightsabers in the Battle of Geonosis. In the scene, a bunch of random Jedi warriors are fighting, holding lightsabers with the familiar blue and green colors any *Star Wars* fan would expect.

But somewhere deep in the mix, I caught sight of something different and did a double take. A purple band of light came in and out of view, and I said, "That's badass! Who's mowing down battle droids with a purple lightsaber?"

The Jedi on the other end of that purple lightsaber was, of course, Mace Windu, played by the incomparable Samuel L. Jackson. It turns out that his purple lightsaber was designed by Jackson to elicit precisely the reaction I experienced. The idea of having Mace fight using a purple lightsaber was, in fact, the actor's own idea.

Several magazines quote Jackson as saying, "We had this big arena, this fight scene with all these Jedi and they're fightin' or whatever. And I was like, well shit, I wanna be able to find myself in this big ol' scene. So I said to George, "You think maybe I can get a purple lightsaber?""

He just...asked! Who knows if this tactic would have worked for a lesser actor. I mean, can you picture some unknown guy asking George Lucas himself for special treatment so he could stand out more in the next *Star Wars* movie? It worked because this wasn't just any actor asking for the lightsaber upgrade; it was one of the most well-known names in film, who simply wanted to make sure he (and his fans) could find his recognizable face on the big screen!

So Jackson got his custom-colored lightsaber, and fans got the perfect way to pick him out of the crowd in any fight scene. You might not be able to differentiate the other Jedis from one another if you can't see their faces on the battlefield, but thanks to that purple lightsaber, you can always pick out Mace, even from a distance.

NICHING IS NOT JUST FOR NERDS

What on earth does this *Star Wars* anecdote have to do with marketing? Well, Mace's purple lightsaber perfectly proves a fundamental truth of niching: *when you do something that no one else is doing, you stand out.*

> When you're a *Star Wars* nerd obsessed with niching, these are the kinds of things that run through your brain. Give me the space to daydream, and it's only a matter of time before I'm thinking about *Star Wars*...and probably also relating it to marketing.

As you know (especially if you're on the nerdy side, like me), standing out can be great—but it has its downsides as well. Every coach and entrepreneur loves to refer to niching as the Holy Grail of owning a business, and they always talk about the pros, but they tend to skip over the cons.

I understand the instinct here. When you're selling someone on a new concept, generally you want to highlight all the great things about it. But the reality is that there are both advantages and disadvantages to niching. The pros far outweigh the cons, but those cons *do* exist and we need to address them.

Why?

Because I want to guide you in the right direction. I don't want you to only see the advantages, dive into a niche, and then discover that it won't be beneficial to you. It is a disservice to pretend that everything is sunshine and rainbows when the truth is that there are a lot of sunny days when you niche up... but it can also be dark and cloudy. It doesn't help anyone to sweep these very real issues under the rug.

There's also not necessarily a solution for any of these cons; they are just potential problems you need to be aware of *before* you decide to niche—and definitely before you decide which niche is right for you. As I said, there are more advantages than disadvantages, which makes up for any drawbacks.

But forewarned is forearmed, as they say, so grab your lightsaber and let's get realistic about niching. It's time to take a closer look at the cons.

CON #1: SMALLER MARKET

The first con that I think everyone is aware of is that when you niche there is a smaller market and, therefore, fewer buyers. The very definition of niche means it is limited to a specialized audience. Depending on the specific business niche, the ability to target customers or audiences can be constrained, which affects business growth.

Simply put, serving a niche means fewer customers.

When you're going after a smaller niche, you're giving up the larger share of the market. The biggest associated risk is that if there aren't enough interested buyers, then there's no profit to be made. You can get reports and check surveys of how many business owners are in that market—but ultimately, at some point, you are going to exhaust your market.

Once you tap your market, your options are either to create additional products and services, or to find additional customers. Let me give you an example of what this looks like, using my company. We are very well known for performing SEO services (a niche within the marketing industry) for personal injury attorneys (a niche within the legal industry). If we have clients in most of the major metros, we have reached the extent of our market. Once that happens, to grow the business any further we either have to sell other services or open our existing service up to other areas of the law—other niches.

There can be a flipside to this as well: some customers don't recognize the advantages of niching and are hesitant to work with someone who niches, thus making an already small market even *smaller*. For example, sometimes I will talk to a law firm that does personal injury, criminal defense, and bankruptcy law (so clearly they do *not* niche), and they don't want to work with my agency because we focus on PI. Because they choose not to niche, they don't see the value of working with someone who is an expert in their own field. The lesson here is that not only are you niching, you're also looking for other people who are doing the same in their industry. Just as "game recognize game," expertise also recognizes expertise.

CON #2: WASTE

The second con (which may not be as immediately obvious as the first) is that it can be more difficult and cost you more money to get in front of your target audience when dealing with a niche. It's difficult to target sub-niches with ads and other traditional forms of marketing.

If I want to sell SEO to personal injury attorneys, I can't go through traditional marketing channels to try to rank for personal injury SEO because it just doesn't get typed into Google very frequently. I can't go to Google ads, bid on relevant phrases, and expect a large pipeline of leads (even though there are about 93,000 personal injury law firms in the US,[1] those search terms only get entered about ten times a month).

As much as Facebook and Google ads have advanced from a targeting perspective, they still don't have enough information to be as specific as you'd need for many niches.

---

[1] It is estimated that there were approximately 92,900 personal injury lawyers in the United States in 2021 (somewhere between 5 percent to 7 percent of all lawyers in the United States). https://adidemlaw.com/blog/2019/08/24/size-of-personal-injury-legal-market/

This is especially true for the topics personal injury attorneys use to niche up, like truck accidents or mass torts. If Joe Fried (a personal injury attorney at Fried-Goldberg LLC who specializes in truck accidents) bids on the search term "motor vehicle accidents" (because it gets typed in more than "truck accidents"), his results are also going to show people searching for information about motorcycle and car accidents, mixed in with the truck accidents he's actually searching for.

I also can't do very specific types of marketing, like running a radio ad campaign, because how can I reach all personal injury attorneys? I could buy an ad on sports radio, for example, but are enough PI attorneys going to listen to that station to make the buy worth it? Probably not. There are paid legal directories I can advertise in, but they don't have a directory strictly for personal injury; there's just not enough volume.

Instead, niching requires *relationship building*, because you can't advertise with direct marketing like you could in broader industries. I go to conferences where PI attorneys congregate so I can interact with them in their specific communities. Similarly, Joe Fried has become a thought leader on truck accidents. (We'll look at this concept of relationship equity more in Chapter 6.)

Because your message is so specific, you also have to spend more to acquire clients, whereas if you had that broader audience, the same spend would get you more clients. It's not as straightforward as for a personal injury attorney who might put a billboard on the road and run a radio ad saying, "Hey, I'm a personal injury attorney. If you've been hurt, contact me," and effectively reach a whole bunch of people who potentially need their services.

Now, in many cases those customers you've spent more to attract are actually worth more because you can charge higher fees (or, in the case of a personal injury attorney, you can earn higher contingency settlements)—along with all the other advantages that come with niching, as you'll see in the chapters that follow.

CON #3: COMPETITION

Niching also introduces competition. You may be the first (or one of the first) in your niche, but once you experience some success and people see you're doing well, they might start to think, "Hey, I can do something like that too!"

Look no further than the history of the motor vehicle industry for evidence of this. Before Henry Ford, no one had cars—so he had a bunch of people to sell to. Once everyone had that first car, he couldn't just sell them another Model T; he had to create a different type of car. Remember what I said in Con #1? Once you've tapped your market, you need either more customers or more products/services.

Here's the thing: Ford found a really good niche—say, oh, being the very first car manufacturer—and that invited competition. Regardless of your niche, once you've identified it, others *will* follow suit because of your success; they'll be right behind you, on the trail that you blazed. Henry Ford would have loved to just continue making Model Ts, but he couldn't because Chevrolet and other car makers started coming in. He had to make different cars.

As you can see, these cons can be layered. You can have both a smaller market share and invite competition; it's not just one or the other.

Joe Fried started out as the only personal injury attorney specializing in trucking accidents, and people thought he was crazy. Once he started crushing it—today he's the leading truck accident attorney nationwide—people came out of the woodwork to follow his lead. They just let him figure it out first.

Similarly, Steven Levin (of Levin & Perconti in Chicago) was one of the first people who created the niche of nursing home neglect cases. Now he has legal precedent—and a bunch of competition after his discovery of a good niche.

> Inviting increased competition can certainly be one of the disadvantages of niching—but like most of these cons, there can also be an upside to it. In the book *The 22 Immutable Laws of Marketing*, authors Al Ries and Jack Trout highlight that one of those immutable laws is being first in a market. We don't talk about who made the second car; we talk about Henry Ford being first. There's definitely an advantage to being number one in a particular niche, from a perception perspective.

The other side of this con is that at the very beginning of creating your niche, you *don't* have competition—and having those competitors nipping at your heels, always trying to take your customers, is what makes you better and drives you to grow and innovate.

Henry Ford's Model T was atrocious looking, but that didn't matter when it was the only car that existed. As soon as other companies came along and started making nicer-looking cars like Corvettes, he couldn't get away with just cranking out boxes with wheels. Had he never had any competition in his niche, we would probably be driving something much different—and definitely not as fast.

Similarly, Elon Musk got everybody talking about electric vehicles with Tesla; once he actually made it happen, Volkswagen, Subaru, and everybody else moved to create an electric option. In this way, competition can be an advantage as much as a disadvantage.

CON #4: LACK OF DIVERSITY

Once you decide on a niche, there is a lack of diversity in your work. You are basically doing the same thing and talking to the same people all the time. If you don't have a passion for what you're doing, it can get monotonous.

Let's use a sports example (see, I'm not just a nerd!) and imagine that you had to play basketball all day, every day. Maybe you get burned out, or over time you just feel like life is passing you by. There's no creativity, no learning, no new challenges, and a lack of new experiences. This probably sounds very boring to someone who doesn't play basketball—but the experience is very different for a serious basketball player who feels passionate about the game. Their coaches are breaking down their game, helping them work on different shots, and encouraging them to practice how fast they can move down the court. They're not just playing the same game all day, every day—and you're probably not actually doing the same thing all the time either.

That's not to say that even professionals can't get sick of their niche. Just think about Michael Jordan, who played basketball and became arguably one of the—if not *the*—greatest players of all time. There was still a period where he went to play major league baseball. Perhaps he got bored with basketball and wanted to play baseball for a new challenge, to learn new skills, and to discover a new frontier.

Ultimately, however, it didn't take (you'll note that we don't talk about Michael Jordan as a great baseball player). He's a good example of why this lack of diversity in your day-to-day can be a downside of niching—and that, for some of these cons, there's no solution. It just is what it is, and it bears acknowledging.

I haven't experienced this personally, because I have a super competitive personality, but some creative types might find that doing the same thing feels monotonous. Whatever your personality, if you're not passionate about what you do, you're probably not going to put out a good product—but you're also not likely to consider that niche in the first place.

If the cons in this first chapter talk you out of niching, maybe you don't have the necessary passion for that niche. You need to have passion before you can go in and potentially spend more money to acquire fewer clients. There has to be something there for you that makes all of this worth it.

CON #5: INDUSTRY RISK

Industry risk is another easily envisioned con of niching. Imagine that you were in the cruise line industry when the COVID-19 pandemic hit. All of a sudden, ships were considered petri dishes of diseases and the prevailing attitude was, "Who would ever want to go on cruises??" It didn't matter if you had the best cruise line, with a wicked slide, the best buffet, and an amazing onboard magician—when COVID hit, people were not going on cruises.

Every industry has some level of risk. Many personal injury attorneys deal with a large number of motor vehicle accidents.

Well, at the beginning of COVID, more people were working from home, which meant fewer people driving, which meant far fewer auto accidents—with the accompanying cases and settlements. I'm not a personal injury law firm, but because I sell to them, I was also impacted—when they have fewer accident cases coming in, they have less money to spend on marketing.

Restaurants closed or were forced to change how they operated during the first waves of the pandemic. With that, however, came accelerated technology and forced innovation. Suddenly, Grubhub, DoorDash, and Uber Eats were the lifeline between those restaurants getting business and you not having to decide what to make for dinner again.

Attorneys who previously had to show up in court for everything were allowed to start making appearances via Zoom.

Technological innovations like the ones we saw take off during the pandemic are a double-edged sword because they quickly render aspects of their industries outdated. If you own a bunch of taxi cabs, Uber and Lyft didn't do you any favors. Similarly, those of us of a certain age watched as VHS gave way to Laser-Discs (remember those? I'm dating myself), then to DVDs, and now to streaming. Even mail service is basically outdated because we now do so much digitally.

As you can see, there can be technological risks in choosing a niche. Once we get flying cars, who knows if we'll even need attorneys specializing in auto accidents (I never saw George Jetson and his contemporaries running into each other in the sky). Then, with those innovations, will come a whole new set of problems that we can't even anticipate until they're more of a reality. Some niches will be eliminated with the new advancements—but somebody else will need to niche into solving those problems.

> Again, every industry has its risk—but every risk means that industry is ripe for innovation and disruption. Is that a pro or a con? You decide.

CON #6: PRODUCT PERFECTION

Another potential con of niching is product perfection. Competition in the marketplace requires companies to develop perfect strategies and provide better solutions. Because there are fewer prospects when you niche, there is less room for error. You must be able to provide products (or services) that are exactly in line with what the customer demands.

What this means is you get fewer reps at the plate. You only have so many buyers in your niche, so you can't turn out a poor product because you won't have the opportunity to make up those sales elsewhere. If you're going to call yourself an expert (and that's what you're doing when you niche up), you lose all integrity and credibility with a buyer if you show yourself not to be that expert they expect. Every sales conversation is based upon trust, and the moment they lose trust in you, that sale is lost and your future sales are greatly diminished.

If you take a swing and miss, you risk damaging your reputation in a small market, which means that future opportunities to sell something to those individuals—even if it's a different, better product—will be unlikely. You have to deliver your best at every opportunity, even if you're just getting started. You have to go out there and hit home runs, even when you're just getting into that niche and may not have everything figured out yet.

Here's the kicker: this is true every single time you have a new product or service. Even if you successfully sell your first product to everyone in your market, this disadvantage rears its ugly head with the *next* product. You will have a brand-new product—and a brand-new opportunity to go down in flames.

CON #7: INCREASED EFFORT AND SACRIFICE FOR BUYERS

The final con on our list may be the biggest of all: when you niche, you may make things more difficult for *your buyers* by increasing the amount of effort and sacrifice they have to make. Let's say, for example, that John needs to purchase a watch and a pair of shoes. If he goes to a niched store like Rolex, which *only* sells watches, John now has to sacrifice more of his time and effort to go to *another* store to buy his shoes. It's far more convenient to just go to one store, like Walmart, that sells both.

As another example, if a client of ours wants a full digital marketing campaign, they have to use multiple vendors because we niched up to only doing SEO. So they have more meetings, more points of contact, etc.—hence raising the effort.

In fact, this is the exact reason Walmart introduced selling groceries at their stores. Sam Walton didn't want to sell produce, but he knew his buyers would like the ease of being able to buy home goods *and* their groceries in one trip. It's easier to go somewhere that has everything in one place rather than going to multiple stores...even if those multiple stores may have better individual goods. A buyer is likely to get significantly more value from making two separate purchases at niched stores, but they may choose to sacrifice some of that quality for the convenience of buying both at once.[2]

BUT IT'S NOT ALL BAD NEWS!

When you look at the negative side of niching, you'll see that many of these cons are related. When you niche and you don't have competition—when you're the only one in a market—your product may not improve because competition is what forces you to improve your product. If you have a super small niche— let's say ten buyers, to make it an extreme example—once you sell your product to one of the ten, if it's not good, you've only got nine more chances…and your reputation may already be tarnished to those other nine. You can't just fake it till you make it in a niche; you have to be an expert because you have limited opportunities.

To the best of my knowledge, my agency was the first to specialize in *only* personal injury attorneys, and I had no competitors of note at the very beginning. Our success has caused other agencies to follow not only our positioning, but also our focus. Even though they're not copying the niche exactly, they've seen the benefits of our approach and are modeling many of our behaviors.

Different industries and different markets are going to experience these cons at differing levels. I can't tell you the specifics

---

2   You can learn more about The Value Equation, which includes Effort & Sacrifice as one factor, in the book *$100M Offers: How To Make Offers So Good People Feel Stupid Saying No* by Alex Hormozi.

of your market, your niche, or your subset. I can tell you that, generally speaking, these are the cons that everybody is going to experience at some level.

The smaller your market gets, the faster these cons appear. If you're going to sell SEO in the legal industry, you have tons of law firms to market yourself to...but once you niche into PI, you have fewer firms. If you then sub-niche into, say, mass torts (a subset of PI), you could tap that market even faster.

It's important to note that the deeper you go in a niche, the faster these cons are accelerated—and the greater the risks can impact you.

I don't want to scare you away from niching—but neither do I want you to wander in with blinders on. You now know the potential disadvantages of niching, and the remaining chapters will focus on the advantages to niching up and how to use those advantages, well, to your advantage.

In the next chapter, I'm going to go against a piece of popular advice. Many people (particularly coaches and mentors) will tell you to just jump straight into your niche, but I think in most cases you should go broader before niching up. Going broad gives you an ability to see opportunities that you might otherwise have missed. It's that *awareness* that we'll focus on in Chapter 2.

CHAPTER 2

↓

AWARENESS

After I graduated college, I became a teacher and, to actually make some money (sheesh, I was broke), I started doing affiliate marketing on the side. In my first year, I probably only made a couple Benjamins…but by my second year, my side hustle was growing more profitable than my "actual" career (although, if you know anything about what teachers are paid, you know that's not a high hurdle to clear). I chose to focus those marketing efforts on health and fitness, and I niched into double chins, launching loseyourdoublechin.com largely as a bit of a joke, but also partly because I was overweight.

I fell into this niche naturally. I didn't even understand the pros and cons, but I *did* know that if I tried to make a website on health and wellness, I would be competing with everyone. I discovered, however, that there's not a lot out there about just the double chin aspect. I thought maybe there was something to becoming the "double chin guru."

Something you should know about me is that I get…let's call

it "invested." People around me have been known to call me obsessive, but I like to think it's just that I'm super competitive. If I'm going to bother doing a thing, I'm going to be *good* at it. What constitutes "good" might vary, but at the very least, I want to be sure that I'm doing the best that *I* can do. That character trait reared its head as I started jumping into the double-chin business. I went into tunnel vision mode and read absolutely every word that I could find about double chins. Once I did that, I buckled down and tried to synthesize that information into what would be the most valuable to my reader.

I wrote all about what I had learned, then made sure that anyone searching Google for a double-chin cure would get served up my site. Soon people were coming to my site to read the well-optimized posts I had cooked up on their hideous turkey gobblers. I did my best to provide my readers with information that would help answer their questions; sometimes, that led to a commission through an affiliate product.

In most cases, to lose a double chin, you need to either lose weight or have surgery. You're probably thinking, "No shit, Chris." But what I also found, while diving into this niche, was that there was a massive audience that related to *hiding* a double chin.

Did you know that a large percentage of overweight males grow a beard to hide their double chin?

Little discoveries like that appealed to a segment of my audience. But I would have never uncovered this had I just focused on general health and weight loss content.

"UH, CHRIS, I HAVE A QUESTION"

When I talk about niching up, the two questions I get asked most often are "should I niche?" and "when should I niche?"

Let me answer the first question first, and I'll answer the second by the end of the chapter.

So the first question is, should you niche? The answer is... maybe.

In the beginning, before you decide to niche, you should start broader by gaining more experience in your desired industry. You may not know if niching offers the advantages that you need, or that there is a true opportunity until you really understand the industry or market that you're in. If you just decide to go narrow out of the gate, it could be difficult to find buyers—or to even know which is the right niche for you.

> David Epstein's book *Range: Why Generalists Triumph in a Specialized World* is a great resource that talks about how to be a generalist before you choose your expertise.

Before you niche, you need more experience so you can identify which niche offers the best opportunities for you. Spanish tennis star Rafael Nadal, for example, played multiple sports before identifying that he was better at tennis, and going all-in on that one sport (he's now one of the best players in the world).

When you go broad and gain more generalized experience, you will have more *awareness* about your industry and market, as well as about potential niches. I first got experience in the general legal field before I chose my niche. During that time, I didn't have the best experiences with criminal defense attorneys; quite frankly, many of them were just assholes (don't hate the player, hate the game). Though it's a fine niche profit-wise, I decided to swerve to the right due to *my* experiences.

If I had gone into the niche of working with criminal defense attorneys right away, I would have bypassed the PI niche I'm currently in (which I thoroughly enjoy) and ended up working with people I may not have connected with as well. Now, if I had gone all-in on that niche, it's quite likely that I would have found some criminal defense attorneys who *weren't* assholes (unicorns are rad pets too)…but maybe not—and then I would have been in a niche with people I didn't want to spend my time working with. That's one of the risks.

Look, I get it…criminal defense attorneys frequently have to defend their clients against serious charges (like, y'know, murder). They yell and scream to make their points to a jury, rather than exhibiting the calm demeanor typically implemented by PI attorneys to elicit empathy and get maximum compensation for a person who has been wronged. They tend to have completely different personalities, but if you talk to someone who has never worked in the legal field, they don't see those differences. An attorney's an attorney, right? They'd think that as long as you're working with any subgroup of attorneys, you're fine. These individuals don't have the awareness of the distinctions between the two niches.

> I think some people's negative associations with attorneys come largely from certain subsets of attorneys. If you're dealing with a bankruptcy or going through a divorce, you're probably not going to have a great experience with fond memories. Those specific negative associations elicit feelings and can give all attorneys a bad name because they all get painted with the same brush.

Another benefit of first looking at the broader picture before choosing a niche is the ability to discover whether or not you have a natural competency in that niche. You may see an opportunity for renovating and flipping houses, for example; a lot of people need that service, and there's a lot of money to be made. But even if you identify that there could be an opportunity there, if you are not a flipper (and not interested in becoming a flipper), you're not going to be successful. If you don't have both the passion *and* the natural aptitude in an area, you're not likely to excel.

Awareness is the first advantage of niching, so to get the most from it, we're going to look at getting experience so you know which niche makes the most sense for you. From those experiences, you can gather the data you need to make decisions. Once you do decide on a niche, you can identify opportunities you previously didn't even know existed.

FIRST, GET *A LOT* OF EXPERIENCE

As you now know, before you niche up, you should go broad and gain a lot of experience in your industry or market.

You need to have these experiences, to actually try these areas you're interested in and see how they feel to you. Do you feel a sense of satisfaction? Is it personally gratifying for you? Do you even know what you're doing? And are you good at it?

If I've never tried to rehab a house, I may underestimate how difficult it is, how much time it takes, or how much money everything costs. Similarly, as much as someone may think they want to be a professional football player, do they have the natural abilities necessary to excel in that area? Is the area difficult to get into, or is the barrier to entry reasonable?

Additionally, having those experiences creates self-awareness. Let's say I'm watching baseball on TV, and I think, "Hmm, that looks easy. I bet I could do that!" But then I actually play a game and stand at home plate, trying to swing at a ninety-mile-per-hour fastball, like a toddler at his first T-ball game. Suddenly I see just how difficult the game is. Say you're watching NASCAR and think, "That may not be easy, but it's definitely doable. It's just driving in circles; they just have to know how to turn left!" But once you zip into that flame-retardant jumpsuit and put on your helmet, it probably feels a lot more complicated (not to mention dangerous). I'm not saying you're going to hop on the field at an MLB game or get behind the wheel of a race car; these are just examples to show that sometimes you have to have the experience to understand what it's really like.

Okay, now let's look at a more relatable example—let me tell you how this went for me.

Before starting my agency, I performed consulting for a lot of niches—every type of industry you can imagine, in fact. I experimented and tried a lot of areas to discover which worked best for me. I worked with attorneys, plumbers, an HVAC company, e-commerce, even *equestrian* marketing (though, at the time, I'd never even ridden a horse!). I worked with all these areas and saw that they had a real need, that I enjoyed working in them, and that there was an opportunity to do business.

After having all these great experiences, I then decided I should go all-in on one niche...but which one?

Everyone knows that Google helps most businesses, but I could see that it really helps the legal industry in particular. I was reading articles about more and more attorneys graduating every year—attorneys who would need jobs, thus creating competition. With competition, I knew there would also be even *more* opportunity.

However, I—like many people—used to be super intimidated by lawyers. I thought they were more educated than me and, quite frankly, would be mean. Then I worked at a digital marketing agency in the legal space and had positive experiences with most of the attorneys I met. I found that, overall, they were really nice, and I enjoyed working with them. Without having worked at the digital marketing agency, I would have written off working with this entire group of individuals. Never in a million years would I have thought, "Hey, I'm going to help attorneys."

So I launched attorney-rankings.org, the original name of my business, and offered all of the digital services attorneys need—website design, SEO, social media, and pay-per-click (PPC).

After niching to legal SEO, I was sitting in a conference room in Vistage (a business mentoring group) for my business review. Everyone was very complimentary about the company as they went around giving me advice. A few members suggested, "You need to do this for physicians, home services, and chiropractors."

At first I thought, "They're right!"

So because I didn't understand how much of a benefit the niche was, I expanded into these other areas, which slowed my trajectory. I underestimated what I gained from focusing solely on one industry: learning the nuances, copywriting and answering consumer intent, and most importantly, providing value.

Armed with that new awareness, I returned to the legal vertical pretty quickly. Not long after that, I niched up further into the PI space. Once I appreciated the benefits of niching, it allowed me to understand who I enjoyed working with and who I could help the most. In my opinion, personal injury attorneys get a bad rap, mostly stemming from how they're portrayed on TV. On the whole, I've found that they're in the business to help people, not chase ambulances. You're gonna find trolls and negative individuals in any space; in fact, I've been referred to as an ambulance-chaser *chaser*!

To be fair, I had some of these misconceptions about the industry and the people in it too…until I actually worked with them, had my own experiences, and gained awareness. From there, I learned how to help my specific audience (PI attorneys), gaining a deeper understanding of them on a higher level and allowing me to tailor my specific SEO service directly to their needs.

Embracing a niche involves "choosing a side." You're going to be right for some individuals but wrong for many others…and you have to be okay with that.

Before committing to your niche, get your feet wet. Experiment a little bit to see if it's going to work well for you. Instead of just *thinking* you may want to try something, immerse yourself in the situations you're considering dedicating yourself to.

THEN USE THE DATA FROM THAT EXPERIENCE TO MAKE DECISIONS

After starting my agency, I was listening to a podcast, and Seth Godin was on the episode talking about his book *Purple Cow*. In that book, Godin discusses serving the smallest viable market and becoming remarkable *for them*. Most people think *Purple Cow* is about niching, but it's about even more than that—it asks, "How do you become remarkable?" Well, with focus...and oftentimes, it takes niching to accomplish that focus.

That podcast episode triggered me to analyze our client concentration and see who we provided the most value to. I discovered that 70 percent of our revenue came from less than 40 percent of our clientele, which were those in personal injury law. I had suspected that PI was that niche, but I needed both the experience and the data to actually make a decision.

Having these broader experiences gives you more data and information to make decisions about where to niche. Take a look at your data to determine which of your clients are the most profitable—and who you most enjoy working with. Then use that data to help you make decisions instead of just guessing.

We found a natural correlation: we could gauge the value that we provided through the growth of client firms. When we saw that 70 percent of our revenue growth was coming from less than 40 percent of our clientele, it was a no-brainer to niche up into SEO for personal injury attorneys.

> When I started in legal, I didn't know that there was a sub-niche for personal injury attorneys that was much more lucrative until I actually started to narrow down. Now that I'm in the personal injury space, I know there's a sub-niche of PI for mass torts. You can continue to go more narrow into sub-niches, but you won't see these opportunities as clearly until you actually have these experiences.

Once I found my niche, I felt more confident. There's that old saying, "competency builds confidence," and I definitely found that to be true. I could speak confidently to a prospect because I knew them. I'd had experiences that taught me about who they were and what they needed. That confidence directly translated into better sales conversions and more referral work...and I just liked what I was doing better! (We'll take a closer look at these other benefits I discovered as a result of niching up in the chapters to come.)

Competency certainly builds confidence, but it also creates passion. If you're playing basketball and you're just terrible and getting thrown around on the floor, you might not love it. But if you are good at basketball—raining three pointers with the crowd cheering for you—you probably like it a lot more.

I got more enjoyment out of my work in this niche. It was more fulfilling because I could create value in a way that most people couldn't. When you're selling a service, you want to do right by your client. You don't want to steal from them or do a bad job. It's satisfying to know that you can serve and provide value (of course, you want to *keep* providing that service—people aren't going to keep paying you if you do a bad job). I found that the work I was doing in my niche landed exactly in the center of my Venn diagram of purpose, passion, and profit.

To learn more about this Venn diagram, see "The Hedge-hog Concept" in the book *Good to Great* by Jim Collins.

I finally felt like I had a path. When you're marketing to everyone, you're just kind of flinging paint at the wall. You don't really know where you're going to go, or how to improve your business. Once I figured out my exact niche, I could focus on helping these exact individuals. That created a natural trajectory—like the original timeline on the Marvel show *Loki*, rather than one of the variant branches.

To use your experiences to make a decision about your niche, look at the data:

- Who makes up the majority of your clients?
- Who is most profitable for you?
- Whom do you most enjoy working with?

You may see that the percentages aren't there—that most aren't going to buy your services, or there's not a big enough market. When you look at data, you also have to consider:

- Are there enough buyers?
- Are those buyers willing to buy the product or service you provide?
- What competition is out there? How much is it going to take to stand out?

Knowing what I do now, today I would take a different approach to look for a new niche: I would go to census.gov and research how many businesses already exist in that niche, to evaluate how much competition there is and see how much money I could potentially make.

For example, I was thinking about another niche: funeral home marketing. We all kick the bucket at some point, people are not going to stop dying, and there's an immense amount of wealth in funeral homes. They have recurring expenses, so it's not all project work. It's security. It balances.

Then I went to census.gov to see how many funeral homes there are. Who's out there in terms of competition? How much revenue do they make? Are funeral home owners even going to buy digital marketing?

I discovered that this is a really underserved market. It's not a strong niche because people don't like talking about death; it's seen as taboo. So while there are tons of people wanting to open legal agencies, the competition for funeral home marketing is extremely weak—almost nonexistent.

At the end of the day, however, my chief of staff and I decided not to go into this industry because dead dudes in a coffin creep me out and we like the status associated with working in the legal space. No offense to anyone working in the funeral field, but we didn't have the necessary passion for that particular niche.

Once you have the experiences to know where your interest might lie, you can utilize public data to help make the decision.

(If you haven't had the experiences yet, you can still look at the data, of course, but you might not know what to do with it or where to go next.) This is why pilot programs and beta testing exist—to understand if there's a need or demand, and to get feedback on what can be improved.

To be successful in your niche, you need experience, passion, profit, and data. Ask yourself:

- Is there a market?
- Do I enjoy working in it?
- Do I know how to work in it? (Or, am I good at it?)
- Can I get paid to do it?

At the end of the day, you're not doing this just because you're good at it; you also need to make money.

ONCE YOU NICHE, YOU CAN IDENTIFY ADDITIONAL OPPORTUNITIES YOU DIDN'T KNOW EXISTED

Once you decide on a niche, you will then be able to identify opportunities you didn't even know existed before you made that decision.

In 2018, Naval Ravikant, tech investor and co-founder of Angel-List, posted a tweetstorm about how to get rich that quickly went viral. In subsequent interviews about the ideas he posted on Twitter, Ravikant made the point that, by specializing, you position yourself to take advantage of opportunities that other people wouldn't have, because of your expertise.

He gives this example:

Let's say you're the best person in the world at deep-sea diving. You're known to take on deep-sea dives nobody else will even dare to attempt. By sheer luck, somebody finds a sunken treasure ship off the coast they can't get to. Well, their luck just became your luck because they're going to come to you to get to the treasure, and you're going to get paid for it.[3]

If you didn't specialize, you wouldn't have the opportunity to dive for that treasure...but because you have taken the time to become an expert—by niching—you get drawn into these unique opportunities.

When I started in the legal space, I didn't realize that PI was such a great sub-niche; I wasn't yet aware of the opportunities the industry offers. If you are starting with home services, you may not realize that working with HVAC and plumbing offers a better opportunity for you than working with electricians (that example is completely hypothetical; I don't know about home services or the opportunities in any of those niches or sub-niches).

Additionally, once I knew my path, I could discover who else was on that same path. I think of it like that scene in *Forrest Gump* where Forrest throws on his hat and just starts running. People follow him because he's going somewhere, and they don't know where to go so his destination is as good as any.

When you're serving one client in your niche, they almost surely have friends and coworkers in the same industry. They're on the journey with you. Your staff is on that journey, too. You're all running in the same direction—and that's what creates

---

3   You can find more of Naval Ravikant's thoughts on wealth and luck, as well as a link to the original tweet thread, in this collection of interviews on his website: https://nav.al/rich.

momentum. One plus one isn't two anymore; it's three or four because of the way it compounds. Once you find the area that you're passionate about, that you're confident working in, that attracts people who want to work with other people who are good at what they do and care about doing it, who can bring other people in—that's the Forrest Gump effect. He was good at running, and he cared about doing it. He wasn't out there preaching it; he was just running. That's why people joined in.

In Jim Collins's book *Good to Great*, he describes that journey as being on a bus. You want to get people who don't share your vision *off* the bus and people who do share your vision *on* the bus.

Of course, as we discussed in Chapter 1, by creating that path, you're also blazing a trail for competition to follow. But because they're behind you, they can also push you forward. Think about *The Lord of the Rings*—Frodo has this ring, but he doesn't know anything about it or what to do with it; he doesn't even know where to go with it. As he has experiences, he learns he has to go to Mordor to melt that sucker. People follow him because he has this destination in mind, but it also pulls enemies in behind him—the orcs and Nazgul chasing him make him run faster.

Also, because I was the first one in my niche, I learned things that people who came after me didn't learn in quite the same way, so they didn't have the same awareness. Even though they (obviously) picked a good niche, they didn't have the experiences I did to back them up. They didn't have the data behind their decisions. They could see the profit potential and the opening, but they were not bringing everything we're talking about in this chapter to it.

It looks easy from the outside—they could see that I stepped into this niche and that things were going well for me—but they don't see the work that came behind that.

Sports analogy incoming!

If you've spent the time learning how to shoot three-pointers, you might miss at first, but you'll eventually make the shot. Then, as you keep working at it, you'll make it even more often. Someone watching you, however—even if they stand in the exact same spot and try to emulate exactly what you're doing—isn't going to make those same three-point shots, because they don't have the learning experience behind them.

The people who follow you in your niche may also fall victim to the Dunning-Kruger effect, which is a cognitive bias where people with limited knowledge greatly overestimate their competence. (Remember earlier in the chapter when we talked about how easy it might look to play football or drive a racecar?) When I was a kid playing poker, I thought I was the best poker player ever—until I actually played with a good poker player. (But more about that story in Chapter 3!)

This also happens on the client side. We'll do a really good job on their SEO, and occasionally a client will underestimate our abilities and assume they can do it too. They think, "I know SEO. I've seen Chris do it. I've been in every meeting and heard these reports."

But they're overestimating their abilities because they don't have the actual knowledge. They're not aware that they're not actually good at SEO just because they've seen someone else do it. They'll then either try to do it in-house or get someone cheaper to do it for them—and that dramatically impacts their ability to generate the same results.

Also, if you try to force yourself to do something you're not good at, it's going to be a drain. You're going to spend time and other resources trying to do a passable job at something you don't care that much about—when there is probably something you're already better at, which won't be that much of a struggle.

BUT WAIT, WASN'T THERE A SECOND QUESTION TO ANSWER?

At the beginning of the chapter, I told you that there are two questions you're probably asking right now (that a ton of other people before you have wondered about too).

The first question is "should I niche?" And the answer is still "it depends."

Have you gone broad first, getting a ton of experience, so you have a greater understanding of your industry and market? Have you then used that experience to examine the data, to see what niche may be profitable and enjoyable for you?

If so, then the answer is yes! But the second question is still on the table: "when do I niche?"

The only answer I can give you is that you should choose a niche only after you've had those experiences, *and* you understand what you have a passion for and the competence to do, *and* the data supports you choosing that niche. That's when you will begin to discover those other opportunities that weren't even available to you *until* you find your niche.

Once you have decided to niche up (if that's what's right for you), you'll begin to experience the next advantage: becoming an expert in your niche. Chapter 3 shows you the benefits of that expertise.

CHAPTER 3

↓

EXPERTISE

During the collectible card game boom of the late 1990s, a somewhat niche game called Legend of the Five Rings (or L5R for short) was released to no small amount of critical acclaim. L5R was similar to Magic: The Gathering, but it was unique in the way the players themselves determined the ongoing story of the game's world, through the results of specialized tournaments.

Although I didn't know the term for it at the time, I was successful at playing L5R because I was niching.

The game's setting is a fantasy samurai world loosely based on feudal Japan. As a player, you take the role of the head of one of about a dozen samurai clans, each with their advantages and disadvantages and each with their own colorful name. For example, the Scorpion Clan specializes in trickery and deceit, while the Unicorn Clan is the only one with a significant portion of their military on horseback.

Many players in the game approach it from a generalist perspective. Sure, they may have a favorite clan (or clans), but they tend to sort of...play them all. After all, collectible card games are about continually adding new cards to the available pool, so the "best" clan may change from month to month as new sets are released. And because winning is fun, people obviously like to play with whatever is considered best at the time.

That was not my approach. I chose to play with just one clan: the Dragon Clan. By focusing on just that one area, I could learn all those little details that other people wouldn't notice if they played many clans. After playing thousands of hands, I memorized every single card in my clan. There's no way I could have done that with multiple clans—we're talking about thousands of cards with hundreds of thousands of combinations. I'm good at math, but it would have diluted my focus too much to even try to understand all those combinations of cards.

I ended up being a top-ranked world player and won two state championships in two years. I even got a reputation; I was a known quantity within this world. When people drew my name as their competitor, they would groan, "Oh, man!"

By focusing on mainly playing the Dragon Clan, I put in my ten thousand hours.

YES, TEN THOUSAND HOURS PLAYING WITH DRAGONS

In his book *Outliers: The Story of Success*, Malcolm Gladwell posits the "10,000 Hour Rule." This is the notion that it takes roughly ten thousand hours of practice and repetition to become an expert in any single discipline.

While I probably didn't spend literally ten thousand hours playing L5R (though I spent a *ton* of time playing this game), the time I spent and the focus I gave to this single area allowed me to become an *expert.*

Expertise is important when niching up because people make buying decisions based upon two things: trust and their expectation that the individual they're buying from will achieve the outcome they're looking for. Experts simply have a greater likelihood of achieving that outcome. Look at Michael Jordan—the reason he's held to such a high standard is because if you have him on your team, you're more likely to win that game. Similarly, when a PI firm hires our agency, they are more likely to rank because we're the experts in the field.

Why is this important? Well, when you are an expert in a niche, you gain two of the primary motivators we, as humans, all share: wealth and status.

Naval Ravikant, the entrepreneur and investor who co-founded AngelList, says that wealth is *not* a zero-sum game—anyone and everyone can be wealthy—whereas status *is* a zero-sum game. There's one winner, and everyone else loses. Think about politics: there's a winner and a loser. Same with sports, particularly individual sports. Trials. Even card games like L5R, for that matter. Status is pushed on us heavily in American society, in everything from your chosen industry to the clothes you wear and the car you drive; even the phone you use is a status symbol.

Once you understand that everyone wants both wealth and status, you can see how becoming an expert delivers both. You are the best at what you do, so you can charge more. (This also is the topic of Chapter 4.) And, you are *the best*—the winner—and people want to work with and buy from the best.

> If you think about it—and if you're honest with yourself—you can likely acknowledge that you picked up this book because you are interested in niching, probably for one or both of these reasons. It's okay to admit you want wealth and status. We all do!

Niching up also brings status because you are going against the norm. Most people think you should go for the largest market possible, to make the easiest sales, instead of intentionally limiting your customer base. Doing so actually elevates your status, however, because now you seem exclusive. Seth Godin suggests thinking of it as having a lock. If a ton of keys can open that lock, the keys are not very valuable. But if only one key can open that lock, how much would that key be worth? (Answer: as much as the individual with the lock is willing to pay.) Some experts elevate themselves to a point where they are the *only ones* who can achieve the desired outcome in their niche, and—to connect both status and wealth—if you want the outcome badly enough, you're willing to pay for it.

Additionally, it is difficult to niche up and become an expert so you stand out because you're making sacrifices most other people aren't willing to make. Even when you have natural abilities in your niche, it's not easy. You have to practice, put in the hours and the effort, and put yourself out there. It's certainly not fast; no one becomes an expert overnight.

If you have heart problems and need emergency heart surgery, you're probably not going to ask the heart surgeon how much it costs or shop around too much. You're going to pay whatever it takes to keep you alive because that's the most important outcome. On the other hand, if you have the time and opportunity to choose your heart surgeon, you'll probably ask around to figure out who is the *best* heart surgeon available to you. Who has been operating the longest? Who has done this exact surgery the most times, with the greatest record of success? You don't just want anyone; you want the expert.

PERCEIVED VERSUS ACTUAL EXPERTISE

Niching brings two types of expertise: perceived expertise and actual expertise.

Perceived expertise comes when someone looks at you and assumes that if you choose to do only one thing, you're probably good at that one thing (because why would you choose to do something you're bad at?). If you're going to hire that heart surgeon, they're a specialized doctor—they've put in their time getting their medical training to achieve that status—so there's a perception that they're a great heart surgeon, even if you don't really have solid evidence that they're actually any good at heart surgery at all.

Actual expertise comes when you actually become an expert. You dedicate your time and effort to learning and becoming the best in one area. You give it all your focus and go the extra mile to stand out from the crowd.

Going from being a perceived expert to an actual expert requires focus. When you initially delve into an industry, you learn a lot of things. But to become an expert, you recognize that you can't get to that level in all of those things so you focus—or niche up—into one, specific, smaller area, which gives you the potential to become the best in that area.

One of the most powerful elements to niching is the focus and extreme attention to be the best at this one thing. When Steve Jobs left Apple and then came back, the first thing he did was eliminate a ton of products, to narrow focus on what was most important. However, if he had, hypothetically, decided to expand in several areas at once, creating three different kinds of computers and four different phones at the same time, we might never have seen the iPhone. But he didn't, and because he decided Apple was going to focus 100 percent on one thing at a time, we now have the iPhone that we all know and love.

That was obviously a great decision, but by choosing that focus, they let go of those three computers and three other phones. Choosing to become an expert in your niche comes with its own risks or downsides, and the biggest of those is the opportunity cost to do other things. You spend so much time becoming the best—like Jordan, the best basketball player, or Tom Brady, the best quarterback—time in the gym, time practicing, time playing and establishing that you're the best, and even time spent promoting yourself. But you have to consider if you want to give this time, attention, and focus to this one area—because, if you do, that's not time you can spend anywhere else.

Billionaire investor Warren Buffet says, "Diversification as practiced generally makes very little sense for anyone that knows what they're doing...it is a protection against ignorance." Most of us have this misconception that diversification is a good thing—but if you *knew* that one stock was better than the other, you would absolutely go all-in on that one stock. The good news is that what you choose to do is something that, unlike the stock market, you *can* control!

I definitely have opportunity costs when I'm away from my wife and my kid, but at the same time, life is about being happy...and doing this work makes me happy. It also gives me the opportunity to do more for my family, to give them more opportunities, and that makes me happy too.

TO BECOME AN EXPERT, LEARN FROM EXPERTS

To become the best, you have to learn from the best. To illustrate this point, let me tell you a story about another card game I learned to play—nope, not a nerdy one (well, not *as* nerdy, at least) this time—poker.

I met Ryan Carter, another top L5R (Legend of the Five Rings) player, at tournaments, and I learned that he was doing internet marketing. Eventually, I moved to Florida to share an apartment with him and some other friends and learn internet marketing.

Well, as these things go, I stayed focused on internet marketing and he went off to play poker.

But Ryan didn't just kinda-sorta play poker for fun; he *played* poker. He got a coach and went professional. He even met his wife on PokerStars (where she had been a pro player as well), and they're still married today.

At one point I told Ryan, "Hey, I want to learn poker, too."

So he became my coach, and we played online poker together, day in and day out, for an entire month. That's all I did. I had extreme focus, and I set everything else aside during that time. In that month, I reviewed every hand I lost—and I played something like forty thousand hands because we were multi-tasking and playing multiple rounds at once (which you can do when you play online, unlike if you play live). We ignored the hands I won and talked through those I didn't. What could I have done differently? Did I actually make the right moves and just get unlucky in this scenario?

In case you're wondering: of course I even niched here. I didn't learn how to play *all* the different styles of poker (which all have different percentages, positions, and hand ranges). I learned one game: No-Limit Texas Hold'em, and that was it.

Ryan's birthday happened to be at the end of that month. To celebrate, we went out drinking. The next day, we were pretty hungover. Between bites of pizza, Ryan said, "I'd kinda like to play in this millionaire poker tournament on Sunday."

"What's the buy-in?" I asked.

"Two hundred bucks."

"Eh," I said. "I don't know if I've got it in me today."

Then Ryan made things interesting. "I'll stake you and pay the $200," he offered. "Just give me half of your winnings."

"Okay, I'm in."

I played that tournament and, using everything I had learned from Ryan and from reviewing all those poker hands over the past month, I came in fourth place and won $234,000!

A lot of people say, "Oh, Chris, you're so lucky." What they don't see when they say that is that I gave myself opportunities to be in that winning spot. I didn't just play a couple hands of poker; I played *forty thousand* hands in a month, which is roughly the same amount that a person who plays live table games would play in their entire lifetime.

I got a lifetime of poker lessons in a month. That wasn't luck. It happened because I was willing to eliminate everything else, to just focus on playing poker—on becoming an expert—and because I was mentored by someone who was already an expert himself.

When you seek to get better at something, find someone who is already an expert in that subject to learn from. That is the quickest way to accelerate your learning. As author John C. Maxwell says in his book *Leadership Gold: Lessons I've Learned from a Lifetime of Leading*, "It's said that a wise person learns from his mistakes. A wiser one learns from others' mistakes. But the wisest person of all learns from others' successes."

If I had spent the time to learn how to play a hand properly, it would have taken me so much longer. But Ryan already knew how to play these hands, and he'd already put in so much more time—so of course I should follow his instruction.

Everything comes back to time. Why do we give value to experts? Well, as we've established, it's because these individuals have focused on their craft with their limited time on this earth, which is fleeting. They've put in the time and effort. They're not just saying they're the best; they have the experience and results to back it up.

When you are ready to niche up and become an expert, put in the time and learn how to do it. But if you want to be the *best* and level up both your learning and the time that you put in, then learn from people who already have some expertise in that area. Leverage their expertise to gain the only shortcut to becoming an expert yourself.

You can spend your ten thousand hours learning and figuring it out on your own. You can first learn to evaluate what went right and what went wrong, then learn how to do more of one and less of the other. You'll certainly earn your expertise that way. Or you can still have the focus and still put in time, but also have an expert coach you so that you don't have to learn everything from the ground up.

When Ryan was my poker coach, he encouraged me to read certain books and to watch poker on TV, but we also reviewed all of my lost hands. When I played L5R, I was a part of a mastermind group made up of the elite players, so I got to hear what they were talking about. When I started working in affiliate marketing, I was in the affiliate marketing forums, listening to the people who were already the best.

I had to put in that time getting an education to become a specialist, but I also had to leverage the resources that were available to me. Televised poker is available to anybody who wants to watch it, and anybody can find the books I read to learn how to play poker (though not everybody does, and that's why they're not experts!). But then I also had a resource that not everybody has access to, with Ryan as my mentor. That mastermind group and those elite forums also helped me level up because I looked for the resources I could leverage.

Look not only at the resources anyone can access, but also the opportunities that are only available to *you*, whether that's because of who you know or because you're the only person looking in the right place.

EXPERTISE = EDUCATION + APPLICATION

When I got into playing collectible card games, there were two main games at the time: L5R and Magic: The Gathering (MTG). I didn't like MTG as much because players were required to publicly post their decks if they played in tournaments. The way I saw it, I created that deck, and they essentially wanted to take my intellectual property!

I didn't want to publish my deck for exactly the reason we talked about in Chapter 1: when you become an expert in something, and when you find something worthwhile, you naturally bring in competition. I didn't want my deck to be posted because then a whole bunch of other people playing at a tournament could utilize the exact same resource I was, and I'd essentially have to compete against—and beat—myself. All those hours I put into learning this game, and they wanted to just take it and roll with it.

But here's what I didn't understand back then: even if I gave someone my deck, they wouldn't know how to play it, because expertise is about both education and application.

This is the difference between watching a video or reading about how to hit a ninety-mile-per-hour fastball versus going out there with a bat and practicing hitting fastballs. The first piece is education, the second is application—and you need both to become an expert. Watching the video and reading is helpful because it allows you to see the fundamentals, to visualize what it looks like to correctly hit that fastball. Practicing hitting is also helpful because it allows you to physically learn to perform the correct technique. But putting the two together is what will allow you to continue to improve and ultimately elevate your skill level.

You still have to have put in the reps, play the games, and gain the experience. Learn from the best, but don't stop there. *Use what you learn to level up, until you have put in the time and effort to become the best yourself.*

Many people are willing to put in the time and effort to acquire the education and knowledge portion of this equation but stop short of what's necessary to achieve the application side of it.

Remember the movie *The Matrix*? In one scene, Keanu Reeves sits in a chair and has different skills instantly downloaded into his body. When he opens his eyes, he instantly knows kung fu without ever learning or practicing.

Most people who watch that scene think, "Oh, that's so cool. I wish I could plug something into my head and learn a new skill instantly!" But that's not how life works. That plug-in programming chair doesn't exist, obviously.

At least not until Elon Musk fully figures out his Neuralink brain implants. If he succeeds and you're reading this from the future, how's that neural interface treating you?

You can read all about kung fu, MTG, baseball, or poker, but unless you get out there and practice the moves, the decks, or the hands, you're not going to become an expert.

AS RICKY BOBBY SAYS, "IF YOU AIN'T FIRST, YOU'RE LAST"

From a very young age, my father ingrained in me, "You only play the game to win. Only winning is fun."

My dad was very status-minded when it came to competition (and athletics in particular). As I grew up, I learned to ask myself, "How do I win?"

While I don't necessarily agree with this "second place is the first loser" mentality, I did learn that in order to be the best and win, I had to have complete focus on one thing, whether that was sports or poker or niching. I had to become an expert—and when I did, the status and wealth would follow.

We've already talked about status, so now it's time to focus on wealth. In Chapter 4, we'll look at how becoming an expert means you can charge more—because you're worth it.

CHAPTER 4

↓

PREMIUM PRICING

Let's say, hypothetically, that you have a double chin and you hate it. You need a solution to help you get rid of it. Well, let's take a look at your options.

Option A is to bust your ass, diet, and get a personal trainer to kick the absolute shit out of you every day to lose weight and shrink that pesky double chin. Option B is to opt for a surgical solution, finding a plastic surgeon who specializes in liposuction to suck away the problem area.

(Or option C, as I learned from my first foray into affiliate marketing, is to grow a beard…but not everybody can or wants to rock the face fuzz, so we'll stick with the first two options for this example.)

Which option is easier? That's obvious: option B. In the surgical option, you take a little nap and let an expert do the work. (Obviously it's more complicated than that, and I'm minimizing the risks involved, but you get the point!)

Now, which option costs more? Also option B. Both options rely on an expert—a personal trainer or a plastic surgeon—but the plastic surgeon, in addition to the expertise required to obtain their medical degree, offers something more valuable to *you*, the patient: a faster, easier solution to losing that double chin.

Simply put, plastic surgeons who offer liposuction can charge higher fees because the speed and simplicity of their offer is more compelling.

LIKE L'OREAL SAYS: BECAUSE YOU'RE WORTH IT

In his book *$100M Offers*, entrepreneur Alex Hormozi details what he calls "the value equation." Essentially, the value equation says that value equals the client's dream outcome plus their perception of the likelihood of achieving that outcome (with the least amount of effort and maximum amount of speed).

When you're an expert, your clients are more willing to pay a higher fee because they trust that you have the ability to achieve the outcome they want.

The first reason you can charge higher fees is because your customers are paying for your experience and expertise. You know where to make the incision, hit the hammer, or throw the football. You're not going through the discovery process; you've already learned your skill, and you've already developed your focus.

The second reason you can charge more when you're an expert is *because you're worth it*. You understand the value you're delivering, and your clients will pay more for that value. You are more likely to achieve the outcome they want, faster and with less effort and sacrifice on their part.

> Entrepreneur Gary Vaynerchuk talks about how exper- tise confers value to things. He uses the example that a basketball in his hands is worth nothing (or close to it). But a basketball in LeBron's hands? Well, that's worth a billion dollars.

Another way to think of this is to consider the Iron Triangle, which says that you can have something that's good, fast, and cheap—but you can only have two of the three at any one time. If you want something cheap and good, it's not going to be fast. If you want something fast and cheap, it's not going to be good. And if you want something that's good and fast, call an expert.

When you're an expert, the "good" side of the Iron Triangle is automatic. People aren't going to pay you for your work if it's not good. Because you are *so* good at what you do, that work is going to be completed faster than it would be by someone who is not as good. That means you have cornered those two sides of the triangle, so your work is not going to be expected to be cheap.

When I began my career in SEO, my retainers were typically in the range of one to three thousand dollars per month. Now, because I have a greater understanding of the competition in my industry and how much I need to invest in order to get the outcome my clients expect, that amount doesn't even cover our minimum fees.

So how did I figure this out?

I used every engagement and interaction that I had with my clients to glean information about the value I was providing through data, feedback loops, and retrospectives. I wanted to know if the value I was creating for the client met or exceeded what I was charging them…and if it did, by how much.

When you work with a variety of industries, however, it's more difficult to understand how much you're worth. I work with personal injury law firms, so I understand why an Uber/Lyft accident would be worth more than your typical, everyday auto collision (because Uber/Lyft typically carry higher insurance limits). Oftentimes, there's more value in a rideshare accident, and I recognize that value because I'm in the industry. I also understand what I'm worth, so I don't devalue my expertise.

All right, so I've convinced you that you are worth the premium pricing you can charge when you niche up and become an expert. Great! But how do you know how much to charge—and when to start charging that amount? We'll focus on that throughout the rest of this chapter.

WHEN TO INCREASE YOUR FEES

In order to increase your pricing, you have to first become an expert so that you're worth it.

But in the beginning, when you are learning your craft and still working to become an expert, charge lower fees and create a low barrier to entry. Once the outcomes that you're striving for start to occur more frequently and more consistently, you'll know that you're ready to raise your rates.

Establish a track record of success and, as you do, raise your prices accordingly.

If you want to become a trial attorney, you can't just read books about being in a trial; you have to get in the ring and try cases. (Expertise = education + application, remember?) When you start consistently winning cases, building a history that you can stand on, you can declare that you are an expert in trials—and charge a higher rate. Your expertise will lend itself to higher contingency results and peer referrals (which is an underappreciated aspect of expertise, which I'll discuss in more depth in a later chapter).

This is another reason why I disagree with those people who recommend niching your business right out of the gate. You have to have all these experiences to figure out what you have a natural competency for, to learn what you're good at, and then to discover how to become consistent at achieving an outcome. You can't just declare yourself an expert and jump into a niche unproven (in fact, the best form of social proof is when *other* people call you an expert, not when *you* do).

Obviously, pricing may vary based on the industry, because the niche you choose dictates how much something is potentially worth to your market. If you are Dunder Mifflin, selling paper to businesses in Scranton, Pennsylvania, they're only going to pay so much. If you're selling *wedding invitation* paper, however (which is still, y'know, just paper), you can charge a much higher fee for the perceived quality of that fancy paper (even if it's just going to end up in the same trash can as the junk mail).

> Chris: "Why is the paper industry so hard?"
>
> Michael Scott: "That's what she said."

As you can see, niching even in something as mundane as the paper industry can affect perceived value.

So once you get to the point where you are ready to niche up and declare yourself an expert, raise your fees to reflect exactly how much you're worth.

COLLECT DATA ON PRICES IN YOUR INDUSTRY

Congratulations, you're ready to raise your prices! But guess what? You still have some homework to do. You have to consider how much your clients or customers will pay to get their desired outcome, which means you're going to have to collect some data.

First, you need data to support your claim of being the best. In sports, you can look at stats to tell you who is the best. In the medical field, you can look at doctors' records to see who is the most successful. That data, in my industry, is all the other personal injury law firms that are ranked number one on the first page of Google. If your clients can look up this information, it is going to factor into how much they're willing to pay.

When you play fantasy football, the really good players go for more money because they make your team more likely to achieve the desired outcome of winning. So when you have two hundred dollars to spend on players, you're going to consider their stats to see who will help you the most.

Once you have the stats to support your expertise, you then have to ask: how much are your buyers willing to pay? And what will they receive for that price?

We talked about status in Chapter 3. Well, it's back in play here because when you are an expert and you charge a higher price, that niche also improves your status *and* the status of your customers. You might buy a cheap watch just to tell time, but if you buy a Rolex, you're more likely to achieve that outcome of status because it's an exclusive, high-priced item made by specialist watch manufacturers.

When considering pricing, you have to figure out the benefit that your customer or client will receive—how it will help them achieve their desired outcome. The benefit of a generic pen is that the user is able to write stuff down. On the other hand, a fancy gold-plated pen that comes in a special holder confers status. In fact, it may never be used to write at all, but instead remain only a display piece.

When we buy something, we're not buying a feature, we're buying the benefit, the outcome. To explain this, I'll paraphrase an example given in an episode of the *My First Million* podcast, which put it very well:

If Mario (while running through the Mushroom Kingdom on his way to rescue the Princess) picks up a Fire Flower, it turns him into a new form of Mario, one that can throw fireballs from his hands.

If someone asked me to sell them on the Fire Flower, I certainly wouldn't focus on how it can grow in tough environments or how pretty the petals are. I would (obviously) focus on how merely picking it up enables me to *throw fireballs* and nuke those little mushroom bastards.

The benefit is the whole *point*, man.

You can charge more because you're worth it, but you have to believe that you're worth it. You have to put it out there that you are worth it. You have to show your buyers that you are the best—and they'll believe it (because you are). Then, when you back it up and prove that you're the best, with the data showing your expertise and experience making it more likely that your clients will achieve their dream outcome, they are happy to pay more *and* to have *their* status elevated for paying that higher price to have the very best.

When you're having heart surgery, sure, you want the specialist, the cardiac surgeon, but you want the head of cardiac surgery because they have the additional expertise that has allowed them to obtain that status. Not only that, you want the head of cardiac surgery at the *best* hospital—price be damned.

A word of caution: not everybody is going to be willing to pay what you are worth. That doesn't mean you should lower your prices; that means you are niching correctly! The goal is to find the smaller segment of the market that will pay the higher prices because they also understand the value of the service or product you provide.

TEST WHAT THE MARKET WILL SUPPORT

Of course, you'll eventually hit a point where people—even your biggest supporters—won't continue paying more. At that point, you'll fail to convert because (at least for most of us) whatever we do is not something people will pay literally any amount of money for. There's always a point of diminishing returns.

It's at this point that many entrepreneurs make a critical mistake. The solution is *not* to reduce your prices; it's to *increase the value* that you provide.

You have to test what the market will support, and I think you should do just what I did: continue to raise your fees until you hit the ceiling at which the value you provide is not enough to exceed the pricing...and then increase the value to justify the higher fees.

This is all just about perceived value and math, and that math is tied to time. Time is fleeting and, without trying to get too dark, we're all going to die. So the most precious resource we have is time, and that's what we're all selling, ultimately.

Again, what makes a good offer? You're going to achieve the outcome faster. Why will people pay more for it? Because their time is fleeting, too, and they'd rather spend their money to buy your time. You've put in the time to gain the expertise. If somebody else wanted to, they could probably learn SEO or brain surgery, if they were willing to go back to school and put in the hours. But they're not—that's what they're paying you for!

So they're already paying you X amount, because they don't want to put in the time to learn how to do this, and then they'll pay you even *more* because you're the best one doing it. Seriously, go out there and find out *just how much* clients are willing to pay for those hours and *your* expertise.

WHICH COMES FIRST, THE SELLER OR THE STATUS?

You, the seller or service provider, have to have some kind of status so that people will buy your product or pay for your service to get that status for themselves.

In Jordan Belfort's book *Way of the Wolf*, he says that you have to convince your buyer to have trust in three things: you, your company, and your product.

People put their trust in you because of your status. It's those awards on your shelves, the degree on the wall, the plaques on your desk. Why do you have these? And why do people care about them? Because they are symbols of status, and status declares to the world that you are the best. By being the best, you can charge more because you're more likely to achieve the best outcome.

It's a never-ending loop: first, you have to achieve the outcome. Then you have to be the best at achieving the outcome, to get status. And then, because people see that status and you back it up by actually achieving the outcome faster, they'll pay you more. And then by achieving the outcome even *more*, chances are they'll continue paying you *more*.

Does your brain hurt yet? I know mine does.

Let me put it more simply: niching up creates opportunities and can create abundance instead of scarcity. You would think that shrinking your market means you would have less opportunity to make money, but in many cases it actually helps you make *more* money.

Now you know that you can make more money when you niche by charging premium prices. In the next chapter, we're going to look at another benefit of niching up, which also ultimately leads to higher profits: increased conversions.

CHAPTER 5

↓

CONVERSIONS

My family recently moved into a new home in a new neighborhood. The other night, my wife and I were trying to decide what to have for dinner. I took out my phone and hit the "food near me" button.

As I looked through the list of restaurants in our area, I saw *tons* of fast food places: Burger King, Taco Bell, McDonald's. That was to be expected. Then, out of curiosity, I decided to see how many nice steak joints were nearby: one. Also not a surprise, but disappointing when you really want a premium piece of meat!

Think about these two extremes. Which restaurant do you think has better food? The steakhouse. Which one costs more? Yup, again, the steak place. And who has less competition? You guessed it again! It's the specialized, niche restaurant.

The fast food restaurants have a *ton* of competition. That's why they have to sell a million Happy Meals; they're all trying to reach a general audience. When you're selling a five-dollar combo meal, you have to do massive volume; when you're selling a fifty-dollar steak dinner, however, you only have to reach that smaller subset of people who want that higher-end experience.

I'm not saying one of these is better than the other. If you have a hungry kid in the backseat, you're going to hit the drive-through on the way home. That kid doesn't even want a steak in the first place: she wants a Happy Meal!

But when you want a steak, if you're like me you want a *good* one. You're going to ignore all of those burger joints and head straight for that high-end joint because they know what you want and they can deliver that juicy, meaty deliciousness cooked to medium-rare perfection. You get to undergo a conversion—from hungry to happy—and the steakhouse also gets a conversion by taking you from potential consumer to satisfied customer.

YOU'RE NOT A JACK OF ALL TRADES; YOU'RE A MASTER OF *ONE*

In the last chapter, we talked about the ability to charge premium pricing as an expert in your niche. This chapter focuses on another advantage of niching: having a higher rate of conversions. Even at those higher prices, you will be able to convert more of your prospects to customers because you know what you're worth, you know what it takes to achieve the outcome, and you've shown that you can deliver value. Prospects tend to see that and think, "They cost more because they're worth it."

In general, there are three ways to generate more revenue:

- get more leads
- increase your win-rate
- raise your prices

Where niching really has an impact is on your ability to charge higher fees (as we've discussed) and on your win-rate percentage—winning more leads through conversions.

With niching, as you know, there's a cap on your market. But because you become an expert, because you niche, you can have greater conversions and raise your prices. If you're more of a generalist, you may be able to increase the number of leads, but you'll likely have a harder time converting those leads and raising your prices because you're not seen as an expert in anything.

As we've established, every sales conversation is really a conversation about trust. You make a promise about what your product or service can do, and the person you are selling to trusts you, or your product or service, to deliver on that promise (or not). By niching, you are aiming to show that prospect that you have experience, focus, and expertise in your area, so they are more likely to trust you. Because of that increased trust, you are more likely to convert those conversations into sales.

Even more importantly, you don't just offer promises; you have concrete *proof* that you can give clients the outcomes they want because you have a historical track record of helping people like them. We actually use that as a tagline on our website: "Anyone can make you promises...We can give you proof."

Because you are an expert in that one area, you can also relate more to your target audience. In sales conversations, the prospect often asks, "Who else like me have you helped?" When you niche, *all* of your customers are like that prospect to some degree, so you can confidently say, "We've helped a hundred other people dealing with the same problem you are, and *here's how.*"

That confidence is acquired by understanding your prospect and knowing exactly how to deliver the results they want (in other words, by niching up). That completes the loop: you know what you are doing, so you have confidence; your prospect sees that confidence and develops trust in you; then, after converting them to a customer, you give them the outcome they want; and finally, your confidence is cemented both in your actual expertise (you did the thing!) and in your customer's perception of your expertise (wow, you did the thing for me, so now I trust you even *more!*).

Here's the secret: once you niche up, these sales conversations won't be nearly that difficult for you because you will be spending all your time working in that one area, with the same customer base. You'll have a fairly precise notion of exactly what a new prospect wants because you're always working with people like them. It's *so* much easier to talk to somebody whose problems you know and understand than it is to sell to somebody who is an unknown quantity because they come from a wider, more generalized customer base.

If I help somebody with SEO in the general legal industry, I only have an *idea* of what they want. But because I specialize in working with PI attorneys, I know *exactly* how to help them because I have legitimately worked with hundreds of other PI attorneys. There may be some small differences (e.g., practice areas, locations) in what they need, but overall, they're doing basically the same thing as everyone else I work with.

Think about choosing characters to play Dungeons & Dragons. When you see someone who is a Fighter/Wizard, you don't think they're the best fighter *or* the best wizard; you probably think, well, they can do two things, but they're also mediocre at two things. They're dual class but they only get half of the skills from each. On the other hand, when you are the person who is just the wizard or just the fighter for five or six levels—you're likely *way* better at spells or fighting than the person who is only halfway decent at both.

Additionally, niching up allows you to be more specific, which also helps increase conversions. Because you're solving a problem for one smaller group of people, for whom your product or service is designed, you can easily put words to that problem. When a prospect comes to me, I can speak directly to them, as an individual, and target specifically what they're looking for. Rather than saying, "We help businesses rank on the first page of Google," I can say, "We help your personal injury law firm rank on the first page of Google."

Being specific makes you substantially more memorable and creates the perception of deeper expertise. I was on a panel recently, and we were each asked to introduce ourselves with what we do.

The first person said, "Hi, I do SEO for law firms."

The second person said, "I do SEO for family law, criminal defense, and PI."

Then it was my turn. "Hey, I'm Chris, and I do SEO for personal injury firms."

For a *personal injury attorney* listening, there's only one clear choice. I stand out because I can speak directly to those—and only those—individuals. (Let me be clear, the other two agencies are great. My point here is only to show how the way in which you position yourself as an expert in your niche leads to how you're perceived as an authority.)

Finally, when you put all of this together—the trust, the proof, the confidence, and the specificity—niching helps you develop rapport with prospects more quickly, which makes it easier to convert them to clients. If I'm doing a sales call and a personal injury attorney says, "We only do high-end litigation, so we just want serious injuries," and I reply, "Oh, so eighteen-wheelers, brain injuries, birth injuries, wrongful death…" and rattle off a list of what they are looking for, they automatically think, "Wow, he knows his stuff." In fifteen seconds, they can see that I'm an expert in this space and that gives them a pretty good idea that I understand their pain points already.

If you don't have the experience in a niche, most of the time you can't do that. By niching, you show that not only are you a part of their world, you've intentionally *chosen* to *become* part of that world. The prospect sees that you understand their problem and you know what they're going through or looking for, which makes it even easier for them to trust that your solution works. Then you back that up with a proven solution that you're confident in because you've delivered it to so many other people *just like them*.

CREATE CASE STUDIES AND TESTIMONIALS

One easy thing you can do to increase your conversions when you niche is create case studies and testimonials specific to your avatar's pain points. Use evidence that supports you being an expert so prospects can see how you've removed that pain for your existing clients.

Just getting started? Do the work for free if you can. Everyone has to start from somewhere to move up the ladder in regards to bigger engagements.

It's all about trust, trust, trust.

After you've done the work, have a conversation with your client. Use that information as a feedback loop to improve. When you've reached a point where you have provided sufficient value, ask for a testimonial so that client can share their experience.

It's that simple. Testimonials are easy for people to write: they just have to lay out their experience working with you. It's not intrusive and requires very little coordination.

If you want to create an even more powerful example to show prospects, you can ask your clients if they would be willing to give you a video testimonial. In a video, leads can see the individual giving the testimonial—they can see that it's a real person. They may think that anybody could be writing a testimonial, but when they see somebody's face attached to it, they feel like they're hearing the experience of a real human being who's like them, who used your service and got the same results the prospective client wants.

To go a level deeper, you can also create case studies. A case study takes it a step further than a testimonial because it shows your prospects an overview of the whole journey. A case study may encompass video, proof items, process, and deliverables. Basically, a case study shows where someone you helped was *before* you helped them. What problem or pain point did they have? Then it shows where they are now, *after* you've helped them. How did you solve that problem? What were the results? In the next section, we'll talk about using a client's specific language to fill in these details.

The goal here is to show as much evidence as possible that you've helped a lot of other people, just like the people you are selling to. Share awards, testimonials, and case studies specifically from or about other people in the same world as your prospects.

Just a tip? No one wants to be a case study, but everyone wants to be *featured*. So instead of asking, "Can you be my case study?" which sounds like you might dissect them, consider saying, "I would love to feature you and talk about your story."

When you phrase it like that, how could anybody say no?

WRITE COPY USING THEIR LANGUAGE

Another way to increase your conversions is to write copy using the language people in your niche use.

Words matter. When I write or speak to my target audience, I don't use the word "lawyer." I say "attorney" because that's how they refer to themselves when they communicate among peers. Moreover, we refer to them as "the preeminent attorney" in whatever field. The word "preeminent" is not commonly used in most industries—but it is in the legal vertical.

Get to know your audience's pain points and their desired outcomes, then use their specific language to speak to that pain and promise those outcomes in all your materials. I know most PI attorneys don't just want small, fender-bender auto crashes; they want serious injury cases. When you have a deep understanding of your audience (which is easier to do because that audience is smaller when you niche!), it helps you write copy that speaks to that audience.

Similarly, I don't say "grow your business" or "grow your revenue" in my copy, both because those aren't the words they use and because those terms are not specific—*how* are you going to help them grow their revenue? With my audience, I talk about "signing more cases."

If you were going to write copy for a car dealership, you wouldn't say you are going to "generate revenue"; you would say you are going to "*sell more cars.*" Maybe you'd get even more specific and say, "I'm going to help you sell more used Toyotas." If they sell more cars, they're going to make more money; that should be assumed. Show them that you understand *how* they're going to increase their revenue when you say, "My product or service will help you sell more cars."

This also helps differentiate you when everyone else is talking about revenue and growing their business, but you're speaking to them about the outcome they care about. You're using their language—that's going to make them take a closer look at you, because you seem like the better fit.

This may sound nitpicky, and these may seem like little details, but all of these smaller elements have a compounding effect.

BE CONSISTENT

Another aspect of niching that builds trust, and therefore increases conversions, is having continuity and consistency in your offer and communication.

Blair Enns, author of *Pricing Creativity*, asks you to imagine you went to a new barber. The first three times you got a great haircut, but the fourth time it was *terrible*. You probably wouldn't go back to that barber, right? He didn't give you a consistently good haircut.

Now, your prospect doesn't know whether or not they're going to get a good haircut every time. But when they see you talking about haircuts the same way, using words they know, showing that you understand what they want, *and* they can see the testimonials or other results from people you've helped—all of this paints this picture for them. It helps them understand you are their person.

Again, it comes down to trust. You will have more conversions because the individual is more likely to trust that you're going to deliver the outcome that they're striving for, because you've done it many other times and you have experience in their niche.

#WINNING

We track win rate in our CRM (customer relationship management) software, so I have statistical data to show when our win rate increased, and then I can look at what the common denominator was, what we did differently.

We had great results previously, but when we made the change to niche and really showed that from a public perspective, our win rates improved dramatically—and, subsequently, our fees increased. In 2018, we had eighty clients and we made three million dollars. Fast forward just two years later, to 2020, and we had only twenty clients, but we made six million dollars.

Sales calls became even easier when we started converting at the higher rate. They were more consistent. When almost every call is the same, we were better prepared and able to craft a better presentation with a better offer—one that better helps our target audience because we were no longer solving for an average of everyone; we were solving for a specific individual. We knew what their pain point was, so we knew how to create an offer that spoke to that pain point.

As an example, spam is very prevalent in the legal vertical, so we had to hire dedicated employees to fight spam. That made our offer better because we were proactively reporting spam to help our clients move up in search engine results. Spam is not as much of a problem in most other industries, so if we weren't in this niche, we wouldn't have known what a problem it is for our audience, let alone have a plan to address it. But because we know our industry, we know that it's a problem and already have a plan in place, so we can talk about that in sales conversations, leading to more trust and higher conversions.

When you get to know your niche, you can similarly get to

know your customers, plan ahead for problems you know they will have, and build trust even *before* they become customers.

Creating more trust also leads to another benefit: better relationships. Chapter 6 will show how your relationships can become currency.

CHAPTER 6

↓

RELATIONSHIP EQUITY

Have you seen the show *Justified*? It's a Western-style modern crime drama starring Timothy Olyphant as a federal marshal named Raylan Givens. (Mild spoilers ahead!)

There's a scene in the first episode of season four where Givens has captured a fugitive named Jody Adair and is transporting him in the marshal's car while Adair complains nonstop. Givens is on a call when Adair starts up again, saying, "I think my arm's falling asleep."

"Stop talking," Givens says.

Incredulous, Adair responds, "I'm not gonna stop talking!" He continues, "Hey, you gonna have to turn me in unharmed, or you gonna catch some shit."

Givens slams on the brakes, causing Adair to smack his head on the dashboard. Then he says, "You know what your problem is? You got no self-awareness. You think trying to do right by your children excuses everything—even killing men."

Adair replies, "They were heroin dealers. If they'd just given up their money, none of this would have happened."

"Every problem, that's someone else's fault." Then Givers delivers one of the most memorable lines of the series: "You ever hear the saying, 'You run into an asshole in the morning, you ran into an asshole. You run into assholes all day—you're the asshole'?" (And then he shoves Adair in the trunk!)

That famous line can apply to niching as well. If you work with one attorney, you just worked with an attorney. But if you work with attorneys all day, you're just like them—and that's your niche.

To put it another way, hanging out with one attorney is just happenstance, two is a coincidence, but three is a customer base.

EARNING INTEREST

Einstein famously said, "Compound interest is the eighth wonder of the world."

When most people read that quote, they automatically associate it with finances and stocks, but there's a different type of currency that also earns compound interest, and that's relationship currency (also known as relationship equity).

According to an *Inc.* article from 2016, the definition of relationship equity is "the distribution of resources between relational partners." The article goes on to say that equity theory "examines whether what the parties in a relationship get out of a relationship is equal to or greater than what they put into it."[4]

---

4   https://www.inc.com/adam-fridman/three-reasons-relationship-equity-is-the-new-lead.html

You can think of relationship equity just like the equity in a house. When you start a relationship with someone, whether personally or professionally, there is a mortgage on that relationship. You owe a debt of value. So you provide value in some way, which makes a payment on that mortgage. (We'll look at ways you can provide value in your niche a little later in this chapter.) As you continue investing in the relationship, you're paying that debt of value and therefore gaining more and more equity.

An important point to make here is that you're not looking to get something out of that relationship immediately; you're giving first. Relationship equity is not about immediate value, it's about long-term relationships, which then lead to that compounding interest.

In his book *How to Win Friends and Influence People*, Dale Carnegie says that the most powerful word you can use when you meet an individual is their name. If you're new to an industry, how many people know your name? Not many. But the longer you're in an industry, the better known you become—and the more relationship equity you develop.

To put it another way, Michael Mogill, author of *The Game Changing Attorney* and one of my acquaintances, says, "Best-known is better than best every time—and the best-kept secret is broke." If people don't know you, then they're not going to work with you, no matter how good you are. The goal is never to be the best-kept secret.

When you are developing these relationships in your niche, you may start by working with smaller businesses or clients. As you gain experience and establish a track record of success, people in your market will grow familiar with you, so you can be seen as trusted. When they trust you, they are more likely to introduce you to their peers. This is how you can become a thought leader.

Those relationships stack, so as you develop and work with larger firms, you get even more trust and continue to move up the ladder. Essentially, you're niching up through your relationships and experience.

All of this creates a world in which you are surrounded by the people you want to work with and those people want to work with you because they recognize you as an expert.

But in the beginning you don't have those relationships. You don't know who the power players are. If I were to start in the home services industry, I know a handful of people I can contact to begin building that momentum. But in the PI space, I know *hundreds* of people.

Additionally, you'll find that, in any industry, the higher up you go, the more difficult it is to get in front of people. If I'm working with a solo practitioner or small firm, I'm probably talking to the owner, but as I move up to these larger organizations, I may talk to a marketing advisor first, then a CMO or different partners, before I really get to the main decision-maker. Getting to the top of that ladder requires an immense amount of trust because there are more barriers and more people who have to trust you, so you have to have even more relationships for them to see your authority.

All of these relationships, this trust, and the authority that you build as you develop equity combine to form your reputation in your niche. But not only do you have to build your reputation, you have to *keep* it as well. As Warren Buffet says, "It takes twenty years to build a reputation and five minutes to ruin it. If you think about that, you'll do things differently."

You are spending a lifetime building your reputation and relationships in your niche. You are not getting a reputation in one industry one day and then moving on to another the next day. This is a long-term investment into those relationships upon which your reputation is built and to generate relationship equity.

How can you do that? That's what we'll look at in the rest of this chapter. I'll show you how to first get to know your people by joining them where they are, then to provide value *before* making a withdrawal from your relationship equity, and finally who *not* to associate with (hint: it's the people who want to take without giving).

I WANT TO BE WHERE THE PEOPLE ARE

In order to build relationships, you have to meet people in your niche—and that means going where those people are.

Join communities or associations your target audience are members of. Go to the conferences they go to, and spend time where they congregate. Once you get to know people and do business with them, your relationship network can grow exponentially. Your clients can then introduce you to their associates at those conferences.

When you're in an industry, it becomes like the Six Degrees of Kevin Bacon. *Someone* knows how to connect you to the person you want to talk to; it's just a matter of finding the right people to make those connections. Once you do, you'll find that the number of people separating you from your target audience gets smaller. If I wanted to talk to John Morgan (who owns the largest personal injury law firm in the United States), I know exactly who to ask for an introduction because I've already gone up the ladder to get to know the person just below him. I wouldn't have to go through six people; I could just go to one.

This again shows the compounding effect of relationships. If you know five people (who you have helped and given value to first, as we'll see in the next section), and they each introduce you to someone at a conference, you now know ten people. If, at the next conference, those ten each introduce you to two people, you've gone from five people in your circle to thirty in the span of two conferences. The more people you know, the more opportunities you have for introductions or referrals (the topic of our next chapter!).

"But Chris," you may be thinking, "how do I know where to find them in the first place?"

Excellent question. When you are first building these relationships, you likely won't know where your prospective clients congregate or what conferences they even attend. So how can you find your people? By using your niching superpower: your focus.

Focus on finding out everything you can about the people in your niche's market. Follow them online, add them to your social media networks so you can see what they're interested in. You'll also learn where they're congregating, which associations they're part of, and what conferences or events are coming up. Discover where they're engaged, what their pain points are or needs they have, and what solutions they may be looking for.

If you see a bunch of people you follow posting pictures on Instagram of this cool conference they're all at, make a note so you can plan to be there next year. By then, you can have even more relationships established so that when you go, your people will be able to introduce you to their networks.

BUT DON'T BE CREEPY

In the next two sections, we're going to look at more specifics about giving value before you ask for anything and how not to be someone who takes without giving, but I want to highlight the importance of both of those here, while we're talking about meeting new groups of people, whether in person or online.

You want to be the person who adds value to a new relationship, the expert in your niche; you *don't* want to be the creepy stalker who takes without giving value. They follow people because they get something from watching others, whether that's information or status by association. (This is why outbound marketing is so challenging—some creep you don't have a relationship with keeps emailing you to try to get you to buy their product.)

So be a fan, not a stalker. A fan gives praise, accolades, and validation. If you start following someone in your niche on Facebook (or Instagram or LinkedIn or wherever your people hang out online), don't be that person who just looks at their pictures all day. Comment on their posts, engage with them, and try to be helpful. If you're in person at a conference, go up to them and have a conversation about a recent win or something positive about them.

But if you want to be Creepy McCreeperton, ignore this advice.

DEPOSIT MORE THAN YOU WITHDRAW

Just like you want to deposit more into your bank account than you withdraw, you don't want to overdraft your relationships either. That means giving more than you take.

You wouldn't walk up to someone you've just been introduced to and say, "Buy my services from me today!" before you've even said hello, right? (You shouldn't do it right after you say hello either, to be clear.) You also wouldn't approach someone and ask them to marry you right after you meet them. You have to court them first. You have to build trust. You don't lead with an ask. You get to know them, develop a relationship, and provide value.

That takes time. You've probably noticed that we've talked about time in nearly every chapter, and that's because time has value. Relationship equity means taking time to meet and get to know all these individuals in your niche. It means showing them, time after time, that you are a good person to know because you can help them—without expecting anything in return (except, wait for it, *their* time).

Only then, after you've helped an individual several times, should you consider making a pitch to them.

In Gary Vaynerchuk's book, *Jab, Jab, Jab, Right Hook*, he describes jabs as the things you do to provide value first so that when you make an ask it's not so weird or intrusive. (He also specifies that you've only earned the right to *ask*—that doesn't automatically mean they have to say yes.)

When you lead with value first, it lowers people's guard. It shows that *you* are a person of value, not just a taker. That can be an opening to a relationship. If you give value, other people are more likely to value you.

I have a podcast, called *Personal Injury Mastermind*,[5] because a podcast is a good way to give value to a lot of people at once. One episode can reach thousands of people, which pays that debt of providing value and therefore gaining equity faster and more efficiently than talking to each of those people individually. The trade-off is that you earn interest at a lower rate. When you build personal, one-on-one relationships with people, you earn relationship equity at far higher rates than you do through one-to-many channels.

When I ask someone to come on my podcast, I'm not asking for their business; I'm asking for them to be a featured guest on my show. That is a value-add because we talk all about them. At the end of the show, I don't ask them to sign up to be an SEO client; I promote their episode. I promote *them*.

Later though, when they're considering who to work with for SEO, I hope that they'll remember me and think, "Chris was nice. He wasn't a sleazy salesperson, and he didn't try to hard

---

5   At pimm.fm, if you want to listen.

sell me. I liked the conversation I had with him, and I'd like to work with him."

WRITE CONTENT

One of the best ways to gain a reputation for being someone who gives value is to write content specifically geared toward the needs of the people in your niche, showing that you really understand them.

Content can mean a variety of things: social media posts, blogs, videos, podcasts—whatever media your niche is most interested in and most likely to consume. Podcasting has been one of the greatest outlets for me to build relationships because I'm giving value to my guests by giving them a stage without asking for anything in return.

In Chapter 5, we talked about writing marketing copy targeted for your niche. Here, you use that same knowledge to write different kinds of content that also provide value. All of it is showing that you know them. You know what their problems are, and you know what would give value to their businesses and their lives.

As the people in your industry consume your content, it is likely that they will come to value you. They'll learn who you are and that you just give away valuable information. That builds trust, which you've seen leads to more conversions (and, as you'll see in the next chapter, also leads to more referrals).

One of the first things I did to start building relationship equity in my niche was to create value on Google+. (In case you don't remember Google+, it was a relatively short-lived social media network where you could create and share lists of contacts, which they called "circles.") I started a law firm networking circle where I curated the list and shared it with anyone who joined and participated.

Even though I wasn't providing a service or selling anything, that list became immensely valuable because I served as a connector for people in the circle. But that list was only valuable because I spent time engaging with all those people on social media, getting to know them, and having them introduce me to more people in the industry.

I built my podcast the same way—meeting a few people who were connected to and trusted by my niche, and building relationships slowly.

Sadly, I got ghosted for my third podcast episode. I had researched the guest and scheduled time with them, and they just didn't show up! However, that's the only time that's happened, because I've since done more than a hundred episodes so now I'm more trusted. My podcast is more legitimate. In fact, while I had to email people to ask them if they would be on my podcast for the first fifty or so episodes, now people email *me* to ask if they can be a guest.

When you develop relationship equity, people will want to interact with you. As you build that reputation of being a person of value, you're no longer just somebody looking to meet other people. Other people get to know your name and want to be introduced to *you.*

DON'T BE A SOUL-SUCKING SNAKE OIL SALESMAN

In the SEO space particularly, certain people are referred to as snake oil salesmen. You don't know them. They travel from one industry to the next, selling their wares. It turns out their solution doesn't actually work—but they don't care because they've already moved on. They're gone, and so is your money.

If you choose to niche, you're choosing relationships. You're choosing to be loyal, to build a strong, positive reputation. That's not to say there are no snake oil salesmen in niching, but they are few and far between because they can't build their reputation. No one trusts them, so it just doesn't work. Niches are small groups of people, and they're going to talk to each other. If someone has a bad reputation in a niche, no one's going to work with them. If you're great, people are going to talk about you—but if you're awful, they're going to talk even more.

I've had to part ways with more than one client because of reputation-related problems that arose while working with them. If we had kept them on as clients, it would have affected our other relationships because we'd be seen as guilty by association for continuing to support them.

Your good name is connected to everyone you work with. Once a client allows their reputation to take that hit, we have a choice: cut them loose, or allow them to drag us down with them.

There are larger, more negative repercussions for being associated with them, so it just isn't worth it because niching isn't only about money. It's about everything we've talked about: relationships, reputation, and value. We never want people to look at us and think, "They do SEO for *that client*. They don't have any integrity about who they choose to work with; that's not the right person for me."

We would run the risk of missing out on working with future clients because they want someone whose values better align with theirs.

As motivational speaker Jim Rohn says, "You are the average of the five people you spend the most time with." Take a look at your niche: you are the average of your five most well-known clients.

Just as you don't want any of your clients to drag down your average, I have to come back to the point that you don't want to lower *their* average either. This chapter is all about how to add, to give, not take away. People don't want to have a relationship with those who just take from them without giving anything in return. (That's why we talked about giving, giving, giving before you even think about asking for something.)

You've probably had the experience, when going to conferences or events, of seeing *that one person* coming in your direction and doing everything you can to avoid them. They feel like a dementor from *Harry Potter*, someone who will suck your soul and drain all your energy—in this case, by wasting your time, leeching any information they can get from you, and sapping all happiness from the room, leaving only dark clouds and coldness. (They definitely didn't get the memo about not being Creepy McCreeperton).

Ask yourself, if you suddenly found yourself transformed into a *Harry Potter* character, who would you want to be: the dementor who sucks the energy and souls from the people around them, or someone like Fred and George Weasley, who give away candy and magic tricks? (Sure, they're turning their audience into magical test subjects, but hey, free candy!)

Or do you want to be someone like Hagrid, who tries to elevate and boost every person (and even animal) he comes into contact with, who teaches people about misunderstood magical creatures, and who will show up with a cake on your birthday to take you away from the horrible family that has been abusing you ever since your parents were killed while trying to save the world from evil?

I may have gotten a bit off-track with that metaphor there, but honestly ask yourself who you want to be. Say you're just starting out, choosing a niche, making a name for yourself, and building your reputation. Once you niche up, develop relationships, and establish trust, who do you want to have around you then? Don't be a dementor, and don't allow yourself to be associated with them either.

RISING TIDES LIFT ALL BOATS

In the previous chapter, we talked about how every sales conversation is based upon trust. When you are better known in your industry, when you give value and build relationships, you are more trustworthy than someone who is an unknown entity. You have a higher chance of converting your prospects and of being introduced to other people in your field.

Well, a rising tide lifts all boats, and developing that relationship equity also lends itself to giving and getting more referrals, which is the topic of the next chapter. When you know the industry, and you know who the people in your niche should talk to, to solve their other pain points, you become seen as even more of a trusted advisor.

CHAPTER 7

↓

REFERRALS

It feels good to help people.

The other day I was pressed for time and had to quickly run into Dollar General to get a birthday card. I got in line behind four kids who were buying chips, soda, and candy. As the cashier rang them up and gave them their total, the first kid paused, dug through their pockets, and said, "Oh no!"

The other kids, who were a little younger than the first, asked what was happening.

"I lost the twenty-dollar bill," they replied.

You could see they were devastated. That twenty dollars represented an absolute haul of snacks for them, and now they were facing a future of scarcity.

Before I could step up and pay for their food, they said, "Be right back," and ran outside to look around the grass out front.

I paid for my card and walked out. Two of the kids were looking in the bushes while the other two were on their hands and knees in the grass, combing every inch of the area for their missing money. All four of them were visibly upset.

I walked up to the oldest kid and asked, "Did you find that twenty?"

"No," they replied sadly.

"Here," I said, and I handed them a twenty-dollar bill from my wallet.

"Oh my God, *thank* you!"

The kid ran over to show his friends, and they were all so *happy*. Twenty dollars is a lot of money to a kid; it represents so many possibilities. (I'm not saying twenty dollars is nothing when you get older, but losing a twenty-dollar bill was a huge deal for those kids at that time, and I was fortunate to be in the position to give them the money.)

And I was happy to help them because I want to live in the kind of world where a person tries to make somebody else's day better instead of worse.

WHO YOU GONNA CALL?

In the previous chapter, I asked you to decide whether you wanted to be a dementor or Hagrid, a taker or a giver.

Consider another question here: do you want to live and work in a world where people are just looking out for themselves, where the client wants to get the most work for the least money, and the person helping them only does the bare minimum and never sends a client to another professional that may be better suited to help them? Or would you rather be in a niche where everyone is trying to solve problems together and looking to help each other, whether that means doing something yourself or connecting someone with the right person to achieve their desired outcome?

I know which I prefer, and it's not even close. Helping people makes me feel good, and I think it just feels better to have positive relationships with the people around me.

A great way to help people and add value (which, as we also saw in the last chapter, builds relationship equity) is to give referrals. You won't be able to solve every problem your target audience has—especially because by niching up you're choosing to focus on becoming an expert in one area instead of just doing an okay job in several areas—but when you can connect them with someone else who *can* solve that problem, guess what? The outcome is the same: the problem gets solved (bonus: now their trust in you likely grows, which helps increase retention).

The best way to create a referral relationship is to give a referral, to give value. If you take every single prospect that comes to you, you don't have any leads to give to other people; you're just taking. When you niche, however, you're naturally saying yes to some things and no to many. Thus, niching allows you to give more referrals because every time you say no, that is an opportunity to develop a referral relationship with someone who can say yes.

This happens with my agency's clients all the time. Just as I was writing this, Daniel Hansen from Hansen Rosasco reached out to say, "Hey, we love your SEO and your agency is doing great on PPC, but we're really struggling with Facebook marketing."

We were able to say, "That's not a service we provide, but you should talk to (so-and-so) at (such-and-such agency). They're fantastic, and I think they'll really be able to help you."

Did *we* solve the problem? Nope, but the problem *will* get solved—and we get to be the ones making those connections. Daniel trusts us, so he trusts that the person we refer him to can solve his problem. In fact, he probably trusts us *more* because we showed that we have his best interests in mind. Someone else could have said, "Sure, we do that," and taken his money, knowing that they're not best suited to solve that problem. Because we were open and honest about what we do well and what we don't (which is just niching in a nutshell), we've reinforced the trust Daniel already had in our business.

Not only that, I'm in this niche so I already know the players on both sides: I understand the legal industry so I know what Daniel needs, and I'm in the marketing space so I know who can provide great social media services. He doesn't have to go research other people doing legal marketing, so he saves time.

There is certainly a *little* bit of effort and sacrifice on his part, in that he'll have a second marketing agency as a point-of-contact (versus just one if he were able to get that service from us). Having said that, do you really expect all agencies (or businesses) to be experts in *everything*? I would argue that an increase in expertise outweighs the minimal increase in effort.

Even if you are not the person delivering the end goal, by giving a referral you are still helping someone achieve their desired outcome. You are still delivering value.

THE BENEFITS OF REFERRALS

The best referral opportunities benefit three people: the person giving the referral, the prospect who is being referred, and the person receiving the referral. The prospect gets help solving their problem, the person receiving the referral will potentially get a new client, and the person giving the referral becomes a trusted advisor for the prospect and earns reciprocity with the person they refer to. This is one of those rare (but truly awesome) win-win-win situations.

Referrals create and build relationships, which can lead to marketing opportunities like speaking engagements, webinars, blogging, or podcasts. One of my top referral partners has a massive distribution and asked me, "Hey, can you write a blog on X?" Agreeing and writing the post meant that they not only promoted it on social media and listed my name as an author on their site, but I also got marketing distribution and an endorsement by this respected company in the legal vertical (my niche).

An endorsement transfers trust from a trusted figure to the person or product being endorsed. We see this when LeBron James or Michael Jordan hold up a pair of Nike shoes. They're endorsing Nike. People trust that LeBron James and Michael Jordan know about shoes because they have been successful in their sport *in those shoes*. If they say that this is the shoe that they wear or recommend, then that trust transfers over from them to Nike.

Not only do referrals lead to better relationships, increased trust, and more opportunities, but they can also help you save money. A typical lead costs money in the form of both marketing and acquisition—but a referral is free. In fact, a referral is likely piggybacking off of money you already spent for a different lead. Once that person becomes a client, if they refer even just one person to you, that's twice the leads for the same money spent acquiring that first person. (But wherever it comes from—and we'll take a look at that in the next section—that referral is always free for you. Note: the moment that you *pay* for a referral, it's not a referral anymore; it's a lead.)

My largest clients have always been from referrals (typically from either clients or peers), and I've even found employees through them. When I have an open position, one of the first things I do is go to the people that work with my agency (my vendors and referral partners) and ask if they know anyone who is great in that position and who is looking for work. I almost always get a few strong candidates.

Ultimately, however, I think that the biggest benefit of both giving and receiving referrals is that you become a connector, and that's satisfying. It feels good knowing that you either got that person in front of the right person to help them, or that you are the person they were sent to, because now you get to help them. As human beings, we *like* to make connections. We like to help people. After all, that's why we do what we do.

You're building that goodwill currency. I don't know if you believe in the concept of karma, but the universe does seem to have a way of returning the positivity that you put into it.

THE THREE TYPES OF REFERRALS

By now you're probably thinking, "That's great, Chris, but *how do I get more referrals?*"

The number one way to *get* referrals is to *give* referrals. You've already seen the benefits of giving referrals, so let's take a look at the different types of referrals and talk about how you can earn more of each.

There are three categories of referrals:

- client referrals
- complementary service referrals
- competitor referrals

Each of the following sections covers one category of referrals in more detail.

CLIENT REFERRALS

First, you can get referrals from your clients.

There are a lot of tactics on how to get referrals (ask for them, have intentional processes and strategies, etc.), but one of the benefits of niching is that you'll be inherently referrable because you're an expert in what you do. If you've delivered someone's desired outcome for them, they're probably willing to refer other people who are like them and who want the same results.

It really is that simple: if you're good at what you do, it naturally lends itself to more referrals.

COMPLEMENTARY SERVICE REFERRALS

The second category of referrals is complementary service referrals, which refers to services your niche audience also needs but that you don't perform. I do a lot of marketing and lead generation, but that's only one component of a business. They may also need help with operations, sales, coaching and leadership, finances, and HR—those are all complementary services in my niche.

You can develop relationships with people who provide those complementary services in your niche so you can provide an end-to-end solution for your clients. Doing so saves your clients time, effort, and sacrifice, because they don't have to find all of those individual people on their own. It also helps them get the best service possible. Full-service agencies may sound appealing on the front end (because they have people that do everything), but because they don't specialize in an area, they may not be as good at some (or all) of the services they offer. When you niche, however, you truly specialize; you can then point to other people who are *also* experts in *their* area and your clients will get better results, all the way around.

That also cements your clients' decision to come to you (and refer you to others!) because not only do you know about your specific niche, but you clearly understand them, their pain points, and even their big-picture outcomes. You know the right people to help them solve problems along their entire journey.

With the other niche service providers, sending them a referral is the epitome of building a relationship. As business owners and entrepreneurs, our goals are to increase and grow our business, so if you directly contribute to those goals for another person, you are adding value for them.

When you first get started in your niche, you may understand that you should give referrals to other people, but not know whom to refer *to*. As you get to know the industry, a natural feedback loop occurs between your clients and who they also work with. You'll naturally learn who may be a potential referral partner for your business and your clients.

Take the time to fully develop those relationships. The greatest risk when making a referral is that the person you're referring to doesn't do a good job, which then reflects poorly on you. Your reputation is at stake, so be sure you know who you're teaming up with.

You may want to consider only giving referrals to other niched businesses. If you send clients to an all-things-to-everyone business for one of the services they need that you don't provide, that business can be a threat to you. For example, if I'm an SEO agency and I have a client that wants PPC, I'm not going to send them to Agency X, which does website design, SEO, and PPC, because they might end up poaching my client. My client also just isn't likely to get the best service from someone who doesn't specialize.

If, however, Agency Y is a PPC specialist and they only do PPC, it's symbiotic. I can send them my PPC clients and they can send me their SEO clients, with no threat to either of us.

Again, the greatest form of giving in business is *giving business*. Everyone wants a pipeline. Everyone wants to grow their business. If you send them referrals, they're going to want more referrals in the future. Chances are, if your service fits the needs of both of your clients, the people you've sent business to are more likely to refer additional people to you than to someone who's never given them any business at all.

Having said that, I subscribe to the mentality of giving without expecting anything in return. Ultimately, it's about helping your client to achieve their outcome.

> Not that you would ever do this, but be aware that there is a big difference between having referral partnerships and colluding to fix prices. Here's how you can tell them apart: referral partnerships create goodwill, and collusion is a crime.

COMPETITOR REFERRALS

The third type of referral is called a competitor referral, and it's exactly what it sounds like: sending referrals to your "competition."

Before you think I'm crazy or call for my head, there are some situations where this makes sense, such as when you have certain forms of exclusivity that prevent you from serving your exact prospects. When that happens, you can develop referral relationships with your direct competitors.

For example, I have a geographic exclusivity contract that prohibits me from working with more than one client in the city of Houston, Texas. I already have a client there, so when I get another Houston lead, I can't help them—but I *can* tell them who else may be able to serve them.

If you have exclusivity provisions in your niche, try to identify those businesses who have similar provisions and who are going to run into the same scenario. That way, if *they* already have a Houston client, but you don't, they can refer the lead to you.

You don't have to player-hate your competitors. You can be friendly with them and evaluate them objectively to determine who the best referral partners are. Referrals are an act of goodwill and truly helping your prospects. Even if you don't have exclusivity conflicts, sometimes it just doesn't work out with a client or they want to work with someone new. It's good to both know whom to send people to *and* to be the person your competitors would recommend in that situation.

When you choose a niche, you're choosing to have a reputation in that niche. The manner in which you treat referral situations has a long-term impact on your business.

Plus, if they know that you're friendly and send referrals their way, it just sets up a better relationship, where they're not trying to aggressively poach your clients or employees—and your competitors may even protect you. We have a referral partner who, anytime a client comes to test the water with them, says, "Oh, you're with Rankings? You're in good hands. Stay with them, talk to them. They'll help you figure it out."

Having that great relationship with referral partners can create a moat, a defensive situation. They're not ruthlessly trying to poach your clients. Instead, they're shoring you up and confirming to your clients that they made the right choice.

I was recently listening to David C. Baker, a business consultant who wrote *The Business of Expertise* and who does a lot of speaking engagements. He asked, "What do you think the number one method is to get more speaking gigs?"

The answer? The other people on the panel, who in many cases are your direct competitors. They likely get asked to speak at other events, and at some point in the future may suggest you join in too. "Oh, you should have Chris on, too. He was great on that panel last week."

People expect competitors to speak poorly about each other, so when that doesn't happen—and then they even take the next step further and ask to invite the competition—it makes both parties look even better.

The reality is that not every agency or business is the same, and you likely won't be able to serve *every* prospect who comes your way. That doesn't mean one of your competitors can't! For example, our agency doesn't do Spanish content. Some of our competitors do though, so if that is something a prospect needs, we want to make sure they can still be helped.

Maybe you're just so busy that you can't help them right away. That's not a bad problem to have! In that case, you have two choices: offer to add the potential client to a waiting list, or give them a few names of people who may be able to help them right away.

Give Them Options

When referring clients or prospects to your competitors, you may want to make it *their* choice whom they ultimately work with. When you're unsure of who is the *best* choice for them, you want to give them options and let them choose for themselves.

If you refer a client or prospect to only one person, you're making the choice for them (and it's unethical if you're not entirely sure of the quality of service that they deliver). You're saying, "This is *the agency* you should use." When you give them several names, it's their choice to evaluate whom to work with.

This is important for several reasons. First, different agencies have different offers, and what's best for each individual is subjective and based on the prospect's specific needs. One may have long-term contracts, whereas another may have short term. One could be cheaper, another could be more expensive. If somebody doesn't have a big budget, they need a cheaper provider.

It's like when you and a friend or your significant other are trying to choose a place to go out to eat. You don't just give them one option; you ask, "Where do you want to eat? Do you want Italian? Mexican? Greek? Sushi?" They're all acceptable options. They'll all feed you, but what do you want? What do you need? What did you have for lunch?

We can niche this up even further. If your significant other says they want Italian tonight, there is then a spectrum of Italian restaurants to consider. Do they want the roman- tic *Lady and the Tramp*' experience? Do they want Olive Garden's hospitaliano, or do they want real, authentic Italian food? Do they actually just want to order a pizza?

Let the prospect then do the due diligence to decide which business best suits their needs.

It puts the responsibility on whichever competitor the prospect chooses to then finish the job and win the business. If the client is choosing between two options, it's up to those two businesses to help the client determine the best fit. But *both* businesses can see that you put their name out there, which creates two forms of reciprocity as opposed to one.

That compounds your ability to get more referrals. If you just send all your referrals to one person, only one business is going to feel psychological reciprocity. If you send referrals to two or three people, then you have more opportunities to get referrals in return.

Look, I know the next paragraph is going to trigger a reaction in some readers…but I want to remind you that most of you started a business to *make money*. That's my warning. Here we go:

If you give only one referral partner your business and load them up on referrals, it could represent additional revenue for them, which can lead to them competing against you for market share in their marketing efforts for future new prospects. So another reason why you want to spread out your referrals to other businesses is to avoid building up threats in your market. They may be great people, but if they're only spending 10 percent of their marketing budget and you give them two million dollars in new business, guess what? They could now potentially afford to market *against* you.

ONLY BAD KIDS HATE SANTA

The issue most people complain about with referrals is that they are often feast or famine. They're unpredictable. That's true: they can be, because referrals are based on serving the needs of prospects.

That doesn't mean you can't tip the scales in your favor.

The best advice I can give you is if you want to get more referrals, be someone worth referring. Be a good person. Do a good job in your business. Be an expert, put in the time, niche up, and set yourself apart. (If you niche it, they will come!)

People get a sense of gratitude from helping other people. If you help people, you're valuable, and other people may want to help you because they'll get a sense of gratitude by doing so. When you give referrals and you're good to other people, you set yourself up to receive goodwill and collaboration in return.

That's why I say that only bad kids hate Santa—because the bad kids don't get gifts! They just get coal in their stocking. (Though with the price of coal going up, maybe that's not such a bad thing.)

If you are a good kid, you love Santa. Similarly, if you are a good person who provides a good service in a good niche, you will find referrals under the tree on Christmas morning.

We've looked at many advantages to niching up, but there's one more I want to discuss, and it ties everything together: Efficiency. Chapter 8 will show you how to create repeatable processes to save time and money.

CHAPTER 8

↓

EFFICIENCY

Think about the very first time you drove a car. You were likely fifteen or sixteen years old or so, and everything just felt so *new and exciting*. That first trip, whether around the block or in an empty parking lot, probably required a lot of concentration: Where do your hands go on the wheel? What are your feet supposed to be doing? How far do you have to turn the steering wheel to move the car? How hard do you have to press the brake pedal to stop the car? Did you remember to check your mirrors? Whoa, you actually have to take one of your hands *off the wheel* in order to click the turn signal?! Is that safe??

Now think about the most recent time you drove a car. Did you consciously think about *any* of that? Probably not. When you've spent years behind the wheel, you get used to it. You understand how to drive the car without having to pay attention to the exact actions you take every step of the way.

What happened between those two car rides? Well, you've put in so many hours driving that you've more or less become an expert. Even more than that, you've done the *same* motions, over and over again, with the same results (allowing for minor changes as you get newer cars with new technology to make it even easier). Driving may have required some real effort when you were a beginner (and that's why your insurance cost more too, because inexperienced teenagers are more likely to get into accidents), but now you have mastered the technique. Not only have you become proficient, you've also become *efficient*.

We can see this efficiency develop in other areas, too. Compare trying to roll your own sushi for the first time to the rolls you get from professional sushi chefs, who have performed the action tens of thousands of times. Consider a cake made by pastry chef Duff Goldman, who has made thousands of cakes, versus baking one for the very first time. Duff's is likely going to be better because he is an expert in his niche *and* because he has developed muscle memory from all that time spent in the kitchen.

BE EFFICIENT

We've talked about all the other pros of niching up that you've read so far, and this concept of efficiency ties them all together. You can be efficient with your processes, but you can also learn to be more efficient with referrals, with relationships, with conversions, and everything else just by gaining experience performing in one area with such expertise. By becoming more efficient, you can make more money, too.

When most people think about increasing profit, they think of raising prices and/or selling more products, but a large—often overlooked—aspect of profitability comes from eliminating waste. Being efficient can decrease your expenses. You can either increase your fees through your implied and real experience, or you can decrease your wasted time, which further increases your margins.

Niching up is a type of lean methodology where you exclude all other industries and just focus on one. By doing so, you also become more efficient because you eliminate redundancies and create repeatable actions.

Let's say that I try to reach a broad market by performing SEO services for professionals. I do keyword research for a personal injury law firm, then I have to do keyword research for home improvement, then for electricians, then physicians, and all the other different industries I market to. I have to recreate that research, from scratch, every single time for each of those different industries. Starting with a blank canvas means spending a lot of time for every new engagement.

On the other hand, if I just do personal injury law firm keyword research, I only start with a blank slate once. The next time I talk to a client who also needs keyword research, I've already done it, for the most part. There may be some small iterations to make, but I can utilize that initial work—and that initial time investment—again and again. It's repeatable.

We've talked previously about Henry Ford and his assembly line, but imagine if he tried to make every car different—different colors, different parts, assembled in different ways. How much slower would that be? From an efficiency perspective, how much time and effort would be wasted? If we look at what he actually did, creating one assembly line to crank out just the model T, he was able to preplan his strategy to be the most efficient and effective.

By niching up, you are able to preplan, too. You can research once and use that effort over and over again—without having to repeat the actual process. Because you work with a solution specific to your niche, that solution becomes more productized, allowing you to eliminate inefficient solutions that don't work for the specific group of people you're trying to help. Instead of having to create multiple landing pages, marketing messages, or sales processes for each industry you could possibly work with in a generalized approach, you are instead able to create one landing page, one marketing message, and one sales process specifically tailored to the smaller group of individuals you have chosen to work with—and whose pain points and desired outcomes you are able to understand on a deeper level because of that decision to niche. If you tried to work with ten different groups, you'd have to stay at a more surface-level knowledge, because you can't dive *that deep* with *that many* people.

Being efficient means using your resources without waste, and one of the most important resources we all have is time. Having the ability to build more efficiencies into your processes means saving more time. There are time-saving components to all areas of running a business, from marketing and attraction, to sales and acquisition, to delivery, finance, and administration. That time-saving is a form of value creation, which can be appended with a dollar amount. You're saving time, but you're also saving effort and energy, all of which means that you're saving money.

BECOME AN EXPERT IN EFFICIENCY

Efficiency also comes from experience. When you first get started, you're probably not going to be as efficient because you just don't know everything. Just like the first time you hammer a nail, you're going to miss it a little bit or it might not be straight. But after you do it enough times, you start to hit the nail right on the head. You gain speed, confidence, and quality in your actions. Because you're working in the same industry, you're going to have those repeated experiences over and over again in your niche, which leads to efficiencies and improvement in quality. By performing the same actions frequently, you reduce errors.

> Kaizen is a Japanese word meaning "continuous improvement." In lean manufacturing, it refers to the elimination of waste and redundancies. One of the best-known proponents of kaizen is Toyota.

In Chapter 3, we talked about niching leading to being an expert or gaining expertise in a specific area after putting in your ten thousand hours. By becoming more efficient, you eliminate waste in those ten thousand hours while adding more value to your time as you achieve expert status.

The biggest area of efficiency for my agency is in operations because we don't have to repeat keyword research. Keyword research is such a time-intensive aspect of search engine optimization: there are thousands of keywords for personal injury law firms alone. Imagine if I had to get thousands of keywords *per industry* across multiple verticals! How would it be possible to do that and be profitable? (Simple answer: it's not.)

But we don't have to recreate these processes from a blank canvas for every prospect who comes in the door. We know exactly where to get backlinks. We know exactly how to optimize their website. We know exactly what cases are worth from a content production strategy. At the end of the day, our personal injury agency is more profitable because we can refine and improve our editorial calendars and processes, repeating those we use most often so we avoid wasted time and duplicated work.

DISCOVER YOUR REPEATABLE PROCESSES

As you get more experience in your niche, start looking for what processes can be repeated because they are the same for all of your clients. You won't necessarily be able to see these areas of efficiency initially, but as you learn more about your industry and customers, you will discover the areas where you can save time.

Turn to your data. Track expenses in your books, profit and loss statements, or accounting software and see if there are places you can reduce waste. Review your operational processes for repeated delivery actions. Measure customer concentration by location and demographics. If you have a process for one part of your business or one demographic, it may be something you can use with another.

BE MORE STRATEGIC

Strategy means trying to forecast what will work, but a lot of that is almost like guessing based upon information that you have gathered through experience and analysis. It's not perfect.

But you can be more strategic by looking at the actions you've taken that have worked for one individual and seeing if you can apply those to more people.

Operations, delivery, or fulfillment is the largest area to consider because that's the car on the assembly line, getting prefabs and put together. The actions you take here to create the good or service are likely performed frequently, which means they will be the most resonant when it comes to efficiencies.

This can also be a place to consider human capabilities versus technology and robotics. Very precise actions that have to be repeated may be better performed using technological programs or robots. But also consider whether certain areas with repeated actions actually have to see those actions performed by you, the expert. Do they require that amount of talent? Are they extremely difficult? If so, you're likely still the best person for the job.

If not, this may be a place where you can hire someone who is not an expert in your niche but who can perform those actions competently so you can focus on the areas where your expertise *is* required. If everything is new and custom, you have to be (or hire) an expert with a wide range of skills. When you have repeated actions, even though you are perceived as an expert, you may not need expert technicians to perform those actions. A high school kid can quickly learn to pull the basket of fries out of the fryer when the timer goes off, whereas it may take years of experience to truly understand all the intricacies in properly putting sushi together. If you own a McDonald's, you can hire the less experienced person, but if you own a sushi restaurant, you likely want the chef who has already learned the skills and who has repeated the process countless times before.

Similarly, maybe there are five people who could build a landing page for your clients (which is a repeatable process), but you are the only one who has spent the time getting to know those clients, so your expertise is required to write about their pain points and your solution using their specific language. That aspect is not something that can be automated or handed off to someone without your skills and knowledge.

There is no shortcut to becoming an expert, but there are things you can do to free up some of your time and mental energy so you can better focus on those areas requiring your expertise.

IT'S ALL A MATTER OF TIME

The overarching benefit of being more efficient—and of niching overall—can boil down to one word: time. That's where value is created. That's also where profit is created. Time is what lends itself to trust, and a transaction is a form of time.

It's all time.

Saving time is powerful. Why? Because all of our time is finite, so it's the ultimate form of value. We're all going to die eventually, so the time we do have is precious and any moment of it that we can save is valuable. If we think of time as currency, niching allows you to save and manipulate time, which makes you more profitable and more powerful than somebody who is trying to do everything for everyone, *even if they're willing to devote more time to doing so*. An SEO agency trying to reach every attorney, physician, and accountant will have to spend so much more time, but will still be so much less effective, than the one just focused on the legal industry.

Even if that generalist is willing to spend the time, is it worth it? They're not going to be as effective because they don't have the expertise, so they're not going to be able to charge a premium, they're not going to convert their prospects as easily (or at the same rates), and they're not going to build up the same amount of relationship equity (so they aren't positioning themselves to give and receive referrals either).

You, however, now know the benefits of niching up so you are ready to save time, be more efficient, and make more profit.

CONCLUSION

Now that you have read about the pros and cons of niching up, I hope you have a clearer picture of just how much those advantages outweigh the disadvantages. But I want you to know that I'm not just writing about niching; I'm actually doing this too, every single day. Let me be clear: I'm not the best at *many, many* things, all of which my wife would be happy to detail. Having said that, I know that niching up has created my own area of expertise, a space where I feel confident enough to tangle with the best.

I want to use my business as a case study, to show you how I niched up and discovered each of these advantages as I went from attorneyrankings.org to rankings.io—not just a marketing agency, or even a law firm marketing agency, but a *personal injury law firm marketing agency*. Let me walk through each of the pros and cons to show you how I made the decision about where to niche, and why that decision was the right one for me.

First the so-called cons, which as you've seen are not always a bad thing:

Smaller Market: I found that 70 percent of my revenue was coming from less than 40 percent of our clientele. Even though our market cap was smaller, that data told me there was a large enough market to support a niched business. Even though this *can* be a con, my profit was showing it wasn't a true con for my niche because there was a large enough opportunity to support it.

Waste: Niching itself actually allowed us to eliminate waste. I didn't offer every digital marketing service; I eliminated the ones that don't help PI law firms and just kept the ones that do, which also meant I didn't need the same staffing capabilities. I was similarly able to eliminate unnecessary expenses in marketing—instead of marketing everywhere and throwing paint against the wall, I'm essentially throwing paint right at PI attorneys—as well as in the sales process, operations, billing, and many areas of our business. (More on that in the section about Efficiencies!)

Competition: In my industry, and especially with the mobile devices we all have in our pockets that allow us to connect with anyone anywhere, clients can choose any digital advertising/marketing agency in the world to work with. But people tend to trust individuals that are similar to themselves, so by focusing on our clients and trying to provide value to that interest group, we've found a way to differentiate ourselves and stand out from the competition. We are the only digital agency that I'm aware of at this time that does personal injury marketing that isn't a heavy media buyer (doing traditional advertising on TV and radio).

Lack of Diversity: I've mentioned this before, but I don't even see this as a con. I have a passion for SEO. To me, it's like playing a video game that pays me. In video games, you're always trying to level up, get more experience, and make more money. I'm doing the same thing, just implementing it in real life. Just like in video games, where you have different obstacles, it's how you overcome it to grow. SEO is a zero-sum game; there's only one ranking number-one position. I enjoy playing to win.

Industry Risks: That doesn't mean that I'm not aware of potential risks of being in this industry. Even though attorneys have been around forever, and individuals are always getting injured (thus necessitating personal injury attorneys, who then need marketing), industry risks are real for my agency. Until people stop being injured, there will be a space for my agency, which allows me to insulate myself somewhat to that risk. However, this is still a con to be aware of. For example, social media marketing used to just focus on Facebook, Twitter, and LinkedIn. Times and attention spans have changed to YouTube, TikTok, and Instagram, etc. Because I am in the digital media game, I can see the shifts coming and am in the position to make a decision to quickly move.

Product Perfection: Because we only work with personal injury attorneys, we are able to survey our clients about their experience and continually optimize for those specific individuals. If I were a digital agency that worked with a thousand different companies across different industries, they would all have a thousand different needs. I get an amazing amount of feedback, which allows me to get better at doing the same thing, making small incremental improvements to continually widen the gap and be the best.

Effort and Sacrifice for the Buyer: Because I'm aware that, from an effort and sacrifice standpoint, we don't offer every type of marketing service, my agency is proactive. We partner up with the best pay-per-click legal marketing agencies, the best media buyers, the best in sales and operations. By knowing our clients, we understand their needs and are able to then find other niche companies, other experts in their craft, to help them. Because I can't help my prospects with everything, I can also give out referrals and set up mutually beneficial relationships. The value in quality and referral relationships outweigh the increased effort and sacrifice in having to talk to a couple different agencies.

When you niche, you can actually turn some of those "cons" to your advantage. Now let's take a look at the pros of niching up:

Awareness: I had to have a lot of experiences to understand where I had competency and where there was demand and opportunity before I niched up into my current industry. I did a lot of affiliate marketing, with more than 100 niche sites. Then I worked for a digital agency that worked primarily with legal but also had other types of clients in HVAC, home services, etc. From that experience, I understood that I worked well with legal, so my first niche was legal marketing. I could have offered digital marketing services to everyone, because I knew where to advertise for attorneys, but I wanted to use my time and capital in the best manner, where the biggest opportunities were. After seven years, when I had enough data to make the decision and was aware of this opportunity to niche up further, I focused in on SEO for personal injury law firms.

Additionally, finding that niche allowed me to learn the specific needs and nuances of that smaller market. Awareness can mean many things, but for our agency it means understanding which digital marketing services help personal injury law firms. There are a lot of marketing tactics, and I am an omnichannel proponent—having said that, certain marketing channels outperform others. We are aware of those that have the highest likelihood of driving leads or improving their brand recognition—but we wouldn't have that awareness without working within a *specific* area of the law.

Expertise: In our industry, pay-per-click tends to be more difficult than in other industries because of the cost per click. A car accident lawyer could pay several hundred dollars per click; it's highly competitive. In order to do television marketing effectively, you have to saturate the market and be one of the top three advertisers—in most markets, that's a six-figure investment. Depending on the size of a personal injury law firm, that may not be conducive to them. We understand where a firm is and what the best services are for them. We can concentrate on providing more value and going deeper with that relationship instead of just guessing, trying to offer everything to see who will buy it. We know what our clients want and need, and we can cater to those needs.

We do SEO every single day. We're talking to personal injury law firms every single day—and we're not distracted by other services or industries. We specialize in search engine optimization. We have SEO curriculum specific to legal. We're SEO masterminds. We have an external SEO coach, SEO speakers. We monitor Google's SEO news on a daily basis. Our entire presentation is continually refined by what's new in SEO. We get to see trends. When you have an entire company dedicated to doing one thing for one market, it lends itself to innovation and true expertise.

Premium Pricing: Most SEO agencies don't understand the quantitative actions needed to get results for personal injury law firms—they don't have the awareness because they've never competed in the industry, so they dramatically underestimate what is needed to get results in a highly competitive market. We know from our experience working with hundreds of PI firms what it actually takes in each market. We can evaluate it on a deeper level. That's why our pricing is higher—not because I just chose to charge high fees. It's because the market demands it.

This speaks to another point about my industry specifically: SEO agencies frequently get a bad rap as snake oil salesmen, and maybe I'm being too generous in my analysis, but I don't think there are very many people in my industry who set out to be deceptive. Rather, I'm of the opinion that the truly competent agencies in this vertical do it so well that an outsider can misinterpret it as being easy to do. Those folks tagged as shysters come into the SEO space with every intention of helping their clients grow, but unfortunately, they aren't adequately prepared for what's required to succeed here.

Conversions: When we speak to a prospect, we're not speaking in generalities of law firms; we're speaking specifically to them and their pains. We understand that a PI attorney typically wants more motor-vehicle accident cases, and we understand the value of those kinds of cases. We understand what keywords they need, the types of content they want. When we talk to them, we are able to mirror our clients and the questions they ask from a deeper level, which lends itself to trust.

Because this is the niche we focus on, we know who they are: I know that most of our prospects are male, in their forties to fifties, former athletes who have competed in sports. Most of them are trial attorneys who are very competitive; they want to win. I understand their desire to win and be the best—and the way I speak to them is completely different from how I would talk to a family law attorney, whose clients are going through a difficult time and have an entirely different persona. I can cater the experience specifically to the PI attorney I speak to—for example, if they are the owner, we focus on the big picture outcome as opposed to the granular details a marketing manager may want.

Additionally, all of our case studies and testimonials are from PI law firms. Our podcast is the *Personal Injury Mastermind*. I know this world and the people in it.

Relationship Equity: Most people think about relationship equity from a financial perspective, but I think about how relationships scale when you choose an industry. For example, when I was getting started in my industry, I worked with solo practitioners and small personal injury law firms. I certainly didn't have the attention of Glen Lerner, Kyle Bachus, Darryl Isaacs, or Mike Morse to invite them to be on my podcast—they had no idea who I was! But as I started to get results and move up the ladder, I was introduced to more and more personal injury attorneys and their friends. Now, for the most part, if I want an introduction to a specific person, someone in my network knows that person and can help get me that introduction. It just scales.

For example, look at the back cover of this book—you'll see blurbs from Joe Fried and Mike Papantonio. Joe Fried is one of the top trucking attorneys in the country, has litigated cases in more than thirty-five states, and co-founded the Academy of Truck Accident Attorneys. Mike Papantonio has written multiple books, made appearances in both film and television, hosts a major conference, and has been inducted into the Trial Lawyer Hall of Fame. Their time is precious, and without that network of relationships I've built up, there's no way they would have come on my podcast or agreed to blurb this book.

Referrals: As of the writing of this book, my agency, rankings.io, offers two services: website design and search engine optimization. That means that we choose to say no to providing every other service personal injury attorneys ask for. Through that focus, we have identified the best specialists for those services, because we still want to provide value to our clients by referring them to the best. We refer to another niched agency for pay-per-click—and that agency doesn't do SEO, so they send referrals back to us. We also refer out video production, coaching, and sales intake. We try to identify and continually improve our referral partners, to help our clients solve the pain points we can't solve for them.

Not only that, when you choose a niche, you become known for that niche. So if another digital agency has a personal injury law firm as a prospect and that agency, for whatever reason, doesn't want to or is unable to help that prospect—if that prospect types in "personal injury marketing," they're going to find us because we've built a brand around this niche, which is a unique selling proposition.

Efficiency: We focus primarily on SEO, ranking a law firm's website on the first page of Google. One of the most difficult and time-consuming activities that an SEO company has to do is keyword research, to determine what the law firm's clients are typing in as search terms to try to find the law firm. Because we focused on PI, we knew that most PI firms wanted the same types of cases so we could create our keyword research once and not have to do it from scratch again. This allowed us to eliminate wasteful activities that weren't repeated very frequently. I could do it once, continually improve it, and have a much better product.

And that's just one example! We have built repeatable processes into every area of our business: keyword research, content strategies, acquiring backlinks for personal injury law firms, creating landing pages, advertising (I know which are the biggest markets and where to advertise for PI law firms), copywriting—even email marketing. Most digital marketing agencies will need to use some logic-based email platform to segment their audience, but because my audience is all personal injury law firms, sure there may be different sizes and price points, but we can speak to one interest group and we can use a simple newsletter to fulfill most of our requirements.

NOW IT'S YOUR TIME TO SHINE

You've read this entire book and learned from my stories—now *you* are ready to niche up and discover the advantages for yourself: greater awareness, better conversions, more freedom, more time, more profitability, a greater reputation, improved ability to deliver results, and more valuable relationships.

We've talked about wealth and status, and niching up gives you both. It leads to greater profit margins, and you also improve your status because you're better at what you do, you are an expert in the space, and you're confident in the results you deliver.

Niching up gives you a sense of gratification, a sense of confidence, and a feeling of goodwill, knowing that you can truly serve the people that come to you, who need your help.

It was my goal, in writing this book, to change the narrative on niching from being about scarcity to having an abundance mindset. Niching is not restrictive; it provides *opportunity*.

In a world of saturation and competition, all of us just want the best. When you niche, you focus all your efforts on doing what is best to help your customers. If you're a business owner and you have a passion for helping a certain market, I would encourage you to go all-in—to think not about the cons of having less, but to look at all the advantages of what niching up can mean for you, from the perspective of wealth and happiness.

If you find yourself competing in a red ocean with a ton of competition, you may benefit from looking at your audience and seeing who you can truly help provide the most value to. Find your own blue ocean—and remember: the narrower the market, the bigger the prize.

If you want to see how I've implemented these niching principles, go to rankings.io.

Follow me on Instagram (@chrisdreyerco) and tag me to tell me how you niche up.

If you're a personal injury attorney, I have another book coming out specific to your interests. In the meanwhile, if you want to hear more about what I stand for, check out my *Personal Injury Mastermind* podcast.

ACKNOWLEDGMENTS

I would like to thank:

- Jenna, for allowing me the freedom to use my OCD as a superpower
- Dad, for always teaching me to play to win
- Mom, for always having my back, even in those rebellious days
- Alicia, for giving me the $15k bootstrap to pursue my dream
- Matt, for helping me find my voice in this book
- Jenny, for pulling it all together
- Ed Dale, for his 30-Day Challenge that helped me learn digital marketing
- The principals at Herrin High School, for giving me the leeway to learn internet marketing in the detention room
- My detention room delinquents, for giving me the push out the door

ABOUT THE AUTHOR

CHRIS DREYER is the CEO and Founder of Rankings.io, an SEO agency that helps elite personal injury law firms land serious injury and auto accident cases through Google's organic search results. His company has the distinction of making the Inc. 5000 list five years in a row.

Chris's journey in legal marketing has been a saga, to say the least. A world-ranked collectible card game player in his youth, Chris began his "grown-up" career with a History Education degree and landed a job out of college as a detention room supervisor. The surplus of free time in that job allowed him to develop a side hustle in affiliate marketing, where (at his apex) he managed over 100 affiliate sites simultaneously, allowing him to turn his side gig into a full-time one. When his time in affiliate marketing came to an end, he segued into SEO for attorneys, while also having time to become a top-ranked online poker player.

In addition to owning and operating Rankings, Chris is a real estate investor and podcast host, as well as a member of the Forbes Agency Council, the Rolling Stone Culture Council, Business Journals Leadership Trust, Fast Company Executive Board, and Newsweek Expert Forum.

Printed in Great Britain
by Amazon

45242937R00088